HOW TO
SURVIVE
IN
CHESHIRE

A SURVIVAL HANDBOOK FOR LONG-SUFFERING LOCALS, CRAFTY
COMMUTERS, NAIVE NEWCOMERS, TESTY TOURISTS, WELL-HEELED
WEEKENDERS, SOPHISTICATED SECOND-HOMERS, FORTUNATE
FOOTBALLERS AND ALL OTHERS DRAWN TO THIS OASIS OF ELITE
EXCLUSIVITY AND BUCOLIC BOUNTY

Geoff Simpson

HALSGROVE

First published in Great Britain in 2010

British Library Cataloguing-in-Publication Data
A CIP record for this title is available from the British Library

ISBN 978 0 85704 042 8

Halsgrove
Halsgrove House,
Ryelands Industrial Estate,
Bagley Road, Wellington, Somerset TA21 9PZ
Tel: 01823 653777   Fax: 01823 216796
email: sales@halsgrove.com

Part of the Halsgrove group of companies
Information on all Halsgrove titles is available at: www.halsgrove.com

Printed and bound by SRP Ltd, Exeter

CONTENTS

Geoff Simpson was born in Kent, grew up in south-east London, lived in Norfolk and came to Hazel Grove in 1975. He is still there.

INTRODUCTION

Cheshire has been my home for 35 years, though I was born a Kentish Man. That means that I came into the world in the Garden of England, but west of the River Medway. So, it is from the perspective of a foreigner, although a long embedded one, that I view my adopted county.

It is not a county that many people think of first in terms of business or tourism.

Yet it contains thriving towns, considerable beauty, provides a dormitory for legions who work in Manchester and Liverpool, borders Wales and offers observers of eccentricity – and wealth - splendid pickings, not least in the "Golden Triangle" to the south west of Manchester.

The Cheshire Plain has some fame as a major agricultural area, yet on the eastern side of the county, the hills are spectacular – the Peak District is not just in Derbyshire, but in Cheshire, Staffordshire and, indeed, Yorkshire too. Then, across Cheshire, is The Wirral, that likes to think of itself as another world and often makes its case.

Motorways affect areas in odd ways. As the M5 ends at Exeter, people now assume that is where Devon and cream teas start. So the modern visitor misses some of the most beautiful of west country scenery between Honiton and the coast at Sidmouth.

Do not make the same mistake about Cheshire. Don't merely hurry north and south on the M6 to somewhere else. But if you do, remember, as you pass, to give thanks to the county, that came to the rescue of the rest of the country in the bleak winter of 2009/10, by supplying all that salt.

Geoff Simpson
Hazel Grove, 2010

ONE
STUMPED!

Some time before I ventured anywhere near Cheshire I was introduced to one of its finest features by a man called Jeremy Hawk.

Mr Hawk, who died in 2002, is perhaps not well remembered now, but for a time he was a considerable television personality, not least as a straight man to the likes of Arthur Askey, Benny Hill and Norman Wisdom. He was also a West End actor and appeared in films including Lucky Jim, The Return of the Pink Panther and the Kenneth More version of The Thirty-Nine Steps.

However Jeremy Hawk also had a manifestation as the host of the Granada quiz show, Criss Cross Quiz and its "Junior" version.

This was how I met him aged 14. I thought that I had done rather well. I had attended an audition in London where I had been one of the few people out of about 35 to score 90 per cent amongst multiple choice answers in a general knowledge examination. Then there was an interview and eventually two of us reached the Junior programme.

My fate was to sit through the recording, one after the other, of the first two shows in a new series without getting on screen. The idea of the show, as you might suppose, was to gain three noughts or crosses in a line. Each square on the board had a subject attached to it – you chose your subject and if you answered the resulting question from Jeremy Hawk correctly your nought or cross appeared on the board. The subjects changed for the next round.

The chap who won the first game was still the champion when I stood beside him as the first contestant in the third show of the series. He was good and I didn't do very well. I got one or two correct answers, but I didn't know that an eagle's nest was called an eyrie and so I was on the defensive.

I had to block the champion and the subject on the relevant square was "Towns". My geography was pretty good, but the question floored me. I hadn't got the faintest idea which town (it could have been anywhere in the world) had rows of shops one above the other.

So Chester was my downfall. The subjects changed again and the question my opponent was asked to win the game was, "How many sides has a rectangle?" On a studio monitor my astonishment at the comparatively undemanding nature of that one was clear. He got it right and I was on my way with a guinea book token as consolation.

Things got worse. I started a fashion at my school for applying to Junior Criss Cross Quiz. I told one chap all the general knowledge questions I could remember from the audition, assuming that he would get different ones. He didn't, was accepted for the show (by then with another presenter, Gordon Luck, in charge), was the champion for a month and won a hand built bicycle and a stack of LPs.

Later that year I was able to inspect for myself the retail facilities of Chester, while on a relatively relaxing day in the middle of a school adventure course, based in North Wales. It was 14 years later that I came to live in the county in which Chester is the historic jewel.

Cheshire and I got off to an inauspicious start, but we came to know each other very well later.

Now I know a little more about The Rows in Chester, said to be a unique system of continuous covered galleries at first floor level – and certainly one of the County of Chester's most attractive and distinctive features. There has been historical debate about whether The Rows evolved or whether they resulted from early town planning. Three out of the four streets that feature The Rows are based on Roman streets.

TWO
GETTING THERE

The trouble with Cheshire is that to some people it isn't actually anywhere. Most folk, including me, would say that it's in the north west, but only just.

As far as I am concerned, driving north on the M6 you pass from the Midlands to the north of England between Keele and Sandbach services. Driving north on the A534 for instance, it is precise. At the end of the village of Butt Lane you travel from Staffordshire into Cheshire, or from the Midlands to the North.

Drive south on the A6 and around New Mills you will see a sign that says "Derbyshire". To me you are now in the east Midlands (and amongst the beauties of the Peak District), though even I must confess that the sometimes rather bleak hills that you can see feel distinctly "northern".

So it's all pretty clear, but people in Cheshire rarely exhibit evidence of the kind of regional or local identity that I experienced when I was growing up in south London, or during the three years in the 1970s when I lived in Norfolk.

Boundary changes haven't helped, but there is still a feeling in some quarters that Cheshire is a place that you pass through or put your head down in when you aren't working in Manchester or Liverpool.

Actually the county, or at least the parts that are historically "Cheshire", do generate strong loyalty, though those that feel the loyalty don't shout about it. You meet plenty of "professional" Lancastrians or Yorkshire people, but nobody ever stakes his or her reputation on being from Cheshire.

So, an early lesson – by all means admit that you are from Cheshire, but say it hesitantly, rather in the way that you would admit to being an accountant. "I'm quietly pleased about it, but not too carried away", is the standard approach.

Accent is much the same. Is there a Cheshire accent? Not one that many can detect, notwithstanding that I'm sure there are people out there who will claim that they can place a voice, with precision, to Crewe or Chester or Tarporley or Marple and there is a dialect as we will discover.

Sometimes the tones more associated with Lancashire do creep in.

There was once a German lady who came to live with her husband in the Stockport area. Her English wasn't great, but she was coping until her cleaner asked her if there was a "dooster" in the house. She phoned her husband at work and he explained that "duster" was what was meant.

Having said all that there are some people who will swear to you that there is Cheshire dialect and here are some of the expressions that are put forward:

People

Dwindle straw – a person too weak to stand up for themselves
Fidge - a fidget
Jagger – a carrier, carter
Ligger – someone who tells lies
Lithermon – a lazy person
Marrow – a mate

Maukin – a woman who isn't as well dressed as she ought to be according to popular opinion

Ripper – a person who impresses

Sowger – a military man

Nature

Ackersprit – Sprouting is apparent on these potatoes

Bonk – Sorry, it means the bank of a river

Brock – badger (of course)

Fairies' petticoats – foxgloves

Hillhooter – what else but an owl?

Hogg – potatoes covered with soil, etc to keep out the cold

Hogs' wool – wool from a year old sheep

Intak – enclosed common or waste land

Pautament – a plague of weeds

Peint – the top of a hill

Provable – crops that over time have demonstrated the farmer's wisdom in planting them

Shoods – husks of oats

Slattery – stay indoors, the weather is wet

Swelling their bobs – It's springtime and the cones are coming along on the fir trees

Appearance

Auvish – acts like a fool

Humpering – walking with a limp

Lammockin – tall, ungainly

Lawp – to eat untidly

Lumpin – big

Nose hole – straight to the point and pretty obvious

Rallock – a garment in tatters

Others

Addling – wages
Back bargain – to go back on a deal that has been agreed
Parl – an argument

THREE
A MAN OF CHESHIRE

A man who loved Cheshire, lived in it, wrote about it and understood its attraction was Thomas Alfred Coward (1867-1933), born in Bowdon near Altrincham. He retired early from the business of bleaching and finishing (of cotton) and spent 30 years as a full time naturalist. Perhaps the book of his that made the most impact was *The Birds of the British Isles and their Eggs* (1920), but, in 1903 he produced *Picturesque Cheshire* and 23 years later when the second edition came out he produced a preface that might well be used today, with little emendation, to give a flavour of the charms of the county. Wrote Coward, "Two decades and more have passed since, awheel, I toured Cheshire and time has wrought many changes in places that I visited. The motor was less popular in 1903 than now, yet some of us, old fashioned like the pots that still attract, enjoy quiet and slow methods of seeing the country; there are advantages in tramping field paths or cycling through shady lanes. The motorist who would follow my track must park his car from time to time, though some field-paths and grass-grown lanes of 20 years ago are now well-paved roads.

"Although I have been over the ground once more I have not revisited all the old homes where I met with kindness and civility on my original tour; the interiors of some have suffered alteration, and too many have changed owners. But there is much in Cheshire, as elsewhere, that defies change and decay and ignores the hurry and bustle of commercialisation. The old church with its associations, the ancient historical country set. The peaceful mere, the old timbered park, may be visited again and again and never grow stale. The tree-crowned sandstone hills, the rugged grit escarpments, the wide open moorlands – the everlasting hills – remain refreshingly unaltered. They are a joy in any weather, at any season.

To make this earth our hermitage
A cheerful and a changeful page
God's bright and intricate device
Of days and seasons does suffice

"A few ancient landmarks have vanished and interesting and beautiful places have been destroyed by the inevitable growth of industrial and residential areas, but elsewhere a wise realization of the value of preservation and restoration has retarded and prevented decay. Yet it is strange to see wireless aerials from timbered gables and motors garaged in time-dilapidated barns; the farmer like everyone else must keep up with the advance."

Coward was a great chronicler, both of Cheshire and matters ornithological. His sudden death, in Bowdon, where he had started his life, unleashed a flood of tributes. The one in the Manchester Guardian declared that, "He occupied the end seat of the end pew, and I have always supposed he chose it to enable him to slip out easily if he heard a particularly attractive bird call, without disturbing the congregation."

Money raised in tribute to T A Coward was used to buy the

land and create nature reserves at Cotterill Clough, west of Manchester and Marbury at Budworth Mere.

He had also explained the history and delights of the Cheshire forests:-

"There were three Norman forests in Cheshire, Wirral, Macclesfield and Delamere, though the last was really double, being the forests of Mara and Mondrem. Little by little this great forest was curtailed; farmers cultivated the land, hamlets grew into villages and villages to towns, while landowners enclosed and annexed portions. The original forest covered most of the land between the rivers Weaver and Gowy, and extended from Frodsham, then on the estuary of the Mersey, so far south as Baddiley, near Nantwich. But a small remnant remained in 1812, when by Act of Parliament the whole was disafforested, portions being sold or allotted to certain landowners and part reserved to the crown as a nursery for timber.

"Ships were needed then to guard against the threatened Napoleonic invasion, but three years later Napoleon was hors de combat and long before the young trees, mostly oak and fir, which were then planted, were mature enough for the navy, the wooden walls of England were obsolete. These fragments of the Royal Forest, rented by shooting tenants, but not cultivated, are the beautiful woodlands which surround us (in Delamere)."

Coward went on to talk of the actions to preserve venison with the enclosure of what became known as the Old Pale in the reign of King Edward III and the New Pale in the 17th century and he also explained how the jurisdiction of Delamere was originally vested in four families, the Kingsleys, Grosvenors, Wevers and Mertons.

FOUR
CHESHIRE ON SEA

When my son heard that I was writing a book on Cheshire his advice was succinct – "Buy a caravan in Abersoch and sit and watch". Abersoch is actually a pleasant little seaside town on the Llyn Peninsula in North Wales. It is some way from Cheshire and I could save the expense of the caravan because there are webcams on the absersoch.co.uk website, but, nevertheless, there was some substance to the advice.

Alternative names for Absersoch are "Cheshire on Sea" and "Bramhall on Sea" and there is a feeling there that you might well bump into near neighbours. It became fashionable in some Cheshire circles to buy a second residence out on the Welsh coast and so, on summer Friday evenings, the 4x4s stream through Porthmadog and Pwllheli and join the A499 that runs out at Absersoch.

You see the same thing in the Channel Island of Jersey on most Friday evenings, when lots of islanders head down to the ferry and off to their second home in Brittany.

At Abersoch the vehicle occupants can enjoy an annual jazz festival, excellent beaches and sailing and have the opportunity to brush up on their Welsh, still very much a living language in that area.

I'm not sure why it should be supposed that going Welsh should be particularly popular with people from Bramhall.

Perhaps it's something to do with where that "stockbroker belt" village fits in the local hierarchy.

People are fond of referring to the "Golden Triangle" which takes in Wilmslow at its most northerly point, Alderley Edge to the south and Prestbury (via the village of Mottram St Andrew) at the south east tip.

This area contains the really snob addresses and here old money mixes with new.

* * *

One tip for those moving to Cheshire, who want to make an instant impression, is to buy their furniture from the delightful, but rather eccentric, premises of Arighi Bianchi in Macclesfield.

It's not just that the firm sells high quality and expensive furniture, after all how would a visitor know that you obtained it from "Argy Bargy" as customers affectionately refer to the retailer? However, one of their distinctively liveried delivery vans pulling up outside your house sends a clear sign to the neighbours that your taste is good and your bank balance is more than healthy.

Currently the fourth generation of the Bianchi family is at the helm and there are 30 showrooms to browse around.

They no longer make their own curtains though – that operation fell victim to the recession in 2009.

* * *

The slightly eccentric air of Argy Bargy is nothing to the activities of some of its potential customers in the Golden Triangle.

I did once drive down the high street in Alderley Edge and noticed David Beckham coming the other way in a sparkling Bentley. He was wearing a woolly hat.

There is absolutely nothing wrong with driving through Alderley Edge in a Bentley and wearing a woolly hat, but, nonetheless, it looked odd. Nearly as odd, I suppose, as the row of 1960s style shops that he was driving past. How on earth did anyone think it was a good idea to plonk that lot down in the middle of the village?

At the time he was perhaps 300 yards from the preparatory school where star gazers could gather to watch their sporting Gods delivering and collecting their children.

One chap I knew had gates at the entrance to his property in Prestbury. A moment of revelation came when they jammed one Saturday morning when his son was due to play in a rugby match.

The fact that the son was able to climb over the gates and into a taxi, hastily summoned, demonstrated both the potential inconvenience of being the proprietor of such gates and their lack of utility when it came to keeping out riff raff.

The Manchester United and Wales footballer Mark Hughes, now on the football management merry-go-round, owned a house in Prestbury (or Mottram St Andrew, depending on your definition of boundaries). In 2007 he sold it to cricket star "Freddie" Flintoff, who was leaving his Preston roots behind. Hughes trousered £1.85 million in the process, or so the Daily Star said.

Freddie then knocked most of it down and spent several more million pounds putting it back together again. Then he and his wife decided to live in Dubai instead and put the Prestbury pad on the market.

The place that gets much of the glory is Withinlee Road in Prestbury, sometimes referred to as "Footballers' Alley", though at the end of 2009 the Daily Mail claimed that there weren't actually any footballers living in it.

However, people do reside there in big houses, where once there were bungalows and farm cottages and they appear to spend an awful lot of money on building work.

"Traditionally one of the wealthiest villages in the region, Prestbury's tradition of discreet money has been swept aside by the bulldozing of old properties on Withinlee ridge – above the equally attractive Mottram St Andrew – to make way for every sort of modern baronial style," declared The Guardian, inevitably sounding rather disapproving.

The paper went on to report that Wayne Rooney of Manchester United and England was in the neighbourhood with a cinema, pool and sports complex for badminton, tennis and five-a-side football and Carlos Tevez of rivals Manchester City was paying £12,000 a month to rent a "carbon friendly" property a few doors away, that extracts heat from the ground for a pool flanked by Armani-design wall panels with an underwater sound system.

Local traders tend to complain that the wealth isn't spent with them, though Colleen Rooney has been spotted in the flower shop and the post office seems to be worth a punt if you collect autographs.

Clearly they don't spend enough though and it really was a shame when the White House restaurant in Prestbury fell victim to the recession. It was very good, with one or two nooks and crannies and even I could afford to go there occasionally.

There was great excitement in the Golden Triangle and amongst those who aspire to it, when Christiano Ronaldo left Manchester United. Up for sale went a house apparently worth

£5m, with a private pool and an exterior that some, no doubt jealous, people likened to the exterior of a Sainsbury's super-store, though whether Sainsbury's was being put forward as a leader in superstore architecture, or the opposite, wasn't clear.

To the *Daily Mail*, the house was "sprawling", though with the consolation for the new owner, that it was set in, "acres of prime land". It was "a palace fit for a WAG", the paper opined.

Alderley Edge has an expensive and well regarded prepara-tory school, but the area is naturally blessed too with inde-pendent senior schools that compete with intensity for the patronage of the well off. They can fill the schools with ease, but they want too the money to fund their projects and the abil-ity to boast in late years of academic high achievers and Eng-land cricket and rugby captains.

So the rivalry between Stockport Grammar School, Cheadle Hulme School and the King's School, Macclesfield often shows itself in all kinds of ways, not least when they play each other in local derbies on the sports field when, at least in the days when the pleasure of family duty took me to the side of the pitch, things could get a little out of hand.

Lurking in the background, ready to pounce on promising youngsters is Manchester Grammar School – regarded by some as a top of the range crammer, but, to counter that ar-gument, they can boast amongst old boys, a recent England cricket captain – Mike Atherton. Also at the school in the same era was another future England batsman, John "Creepy" Crawley.

Cheadle Hulme is less of a mouthful than it was 150 years ago when it started life as The Manchester Warehousemen and Clerks' Orphanage School and things have also changed a little since those days, when the Manchester businessmen who established it regarded its purpose as to educate "orphans and necessitous children".

Now the times are really changing, as a recent breathless announcement by the school shows:-

"Cheadle Hulme School has appointed the first female Head in the School's 154 year history. Lucy Pearson, currently Deputy Head at Wellington College and a Vice Principal of the newly formed Wellington Academy, will take up the role in September 2010. 'I am absolutely delighted to have been appointed Head of Cheadle Hulme School from September 2010,' says Lucy. 'The pupils and the school have achieved wonderful things under the leadership of Paul Dixon and I am relishing the prospect of expanding its reputation and its ambitions, confirming that it is indeed one of the outstanding co-educational day schools in the country.'"

* * *

Perhaps then getting more to the point we are told that, "Lucy brings a wealth of experience to the role. An Oxford University graduate (English Literature and Language, Keble College), she is passionate about co-education and believes that it is every school's responsibility to inspire each child to flourish and thereby realise their potential both within the classroom and beyond. Not only a high achieving academic, Lucy is also a successful international sportswoman. She opened the bowling for the England Women's Cricket Team from 1996 until 2005, achieving a world record in the Second Ashes Test at Sydney in 2003, as well as twice being named Player of the Year. She is also an accomplished musician, being a former member of the National Youth Choir."

Over at "King's Macc", a school that has been around, in different guises, since the 16th century, they are moving with the times too and have been boasting about the triumph of the girls' rugby team, capable of "superb flowing rugby", that has enabled it to walk off with the Northern Schools' Sevens trophy.

Stockport Grammar School, "SGS", now has an impressive frontage along the A6, marred only by Kwik Fit tyres popping up in the middle of it. Their list of former pupils features John Amaechi, who reached basketball stardom in America and Cecil Kimber, the man who built up the reputation of MG cars between the wars.

FIVE
COD FILLETS

Every year in March members of Ecurie Cod Fillet journey to Cheshire, the home of their founding father. Those in the know as to their habits can find them and spot them easily. They will be sat in a corner of a bar. It is perhaps an exaggeration to say that they all have handlebar moustaches, but sidle close and listen. "Was it '54 or '55 when Tubby Ponsonby finished up in that tree on the Col de Turini?" is an exemplifying gambit. Or amongst the slightly younger ones, "That's the firebreak in Hafren (forest) that Russell went down and landed on top of Malcolm."

What you are listening to is the cream of Britain's veteran rally drivers and navigators reliving their glory days, which often involved "visiting the scenery", "having an enormous moment" and suffering accidents that "started at one map reference and finished at another". You will hear them speak in awe of the mountain roads of the Alpes-Maritime encountered on the Monte Carlo Rally in January and the features of the forests of England, Wales and Scotland, some of those remote places amongst the trees are named after the rally driver who ran out of road at the spot. (And if you ever sit in a rally car you will know that you are approaching such a piece of history when you glimpse a vast crowd through the trees and they start beckoning you to go faster.)

Cheshire is a spiritual home to this exclusive club (about 300 members, all by invitation) because the idea and the impetus came from former Manchester fish merchant, Roy Fidler, who lives in Bramhall and whose habit, at one time at least, was to drive around in cars registered "COD 1", "COD 2", etc. He and his late navigator, John Hopwood founded the fraternity many years ago and on and on it drinks.

Their weekend out in Cheshire occurs at the start of March when winter still poses a bit of a threat that can add to the fun. The excuse is the Tour of Cheshire rally for classic cars, founded by a Cod Fillet member Nigel Raeburn and organised by Knutsford and District Motor Club of which he is also a member.

They do claim that anyone who owns, or can get their hands on, a pre-1981 car can enter and enjoy the Tour of Cheshire, but the absolute novice will find the navigation and timekeeping more than a little daunting.

The point came home to me one year when I manned a time control in a country lane near the Oulton Park motor racing circuit and watched a considerable number of competitors motor along a road in the distance and miss us out. On another occasion and rather oddly, the two leading cars failed to visit the control I was at and everybody else found it. Admittedly I was actually in Staffordshire at the time, so perhaps that had something to do with it.

It should be stressed that all cars stick rigidly to prescribed speeds and other legalities while on public roads, though the drivers do let their hair down a bit when it comes to tests round cones in farmyards, the grounds of stately homes and so on.

The Cod Fillet grandees turn out to wave starter's flags, chat to the fans and generally get involved. Some spectators scour the loft for items of 50s and 60s clothes to wear and many people emerge from their front doors to watch the procession of Porsches, Triumphs, MGs, Sunbeams, Ford Escorts and other exotic and less exotic machinery.

If motoring as it was is your thing, join the guys from Ecurie Cod Fillet in Cheshire in March.

That's not the only way of enjoying motorsport in Cheshire of course.

The Oulton Park circuit near Little Budworth has been around for a long time. In the 50s, motor racing from that rural setting was something not to be missed on TV – they even had Formula 1 cars sometimes.

Today, if you go for a walk in the lanes of that part of the county, you will often detect the low hum across the fields that tells you that something is going on at the circuit, perhaps actual racing, perhaps a test day for cars or motorbikes.

I never gave any thought as a youngster to how the features of the circuit got their names – Lodge Corner, The Avenue, Deer Leap, Old Hall Corner and the rest. Neither did I give much thought to the distinctly impressive, if rather sad looking, edifice on the edge of the race circuit grounds that I stumbled across after I came to live in Cheshire.

Now I know a little more. The race track was built in the grounds of Oulton Hall and the Hall had a history. There was a Tudor house there, destroyed by fire it is claimed, sadly a portent of what was to come. From 1715 a new house began to emerge under the auspices of John Egerton. Members of his family continued the work, a wall was built round the estate and landscaped gardens developed. A feature of the gardens is recalled in the "Cascades" bend negotiated by today's car and bike racers.

Money ran low and there was little development in later years. Then came a major fire in 1926, six lives were lost and, it is said, major works of art lost. The hall was partially destroyed and German bombs finished the job off in 1940, a rather unlucky occurrence in rural Cheshire. The sad edifice shows where the entrance to the estate was.

So now we have a splendid and undulating motor racing circuit, another of the corners of which is named "Knickerbrook". Now this can't be an historical reference to the house, can it?

Apparently not. It is claimed , no doubt apocryphally, that tree clearing, using explosives, was taking place in that area of the grounds and a bang disturbed a courting couple who made a hasty exit, the lady leaving at least one of her possessions behind. And so Knickerbrook came to be named and to fascinate generations of youthful motor racing enthusiasts.

The man who took the credit for being the cause of this drama was "Blaster" Bates, a great Cheshire character, who died in 2006 aged 83. Born in Crewe, he served in the RAF in the Second World War and then built a reputation as demolition and explosives expert and story teller. Amongst the achievements of which he seemed particularly proud was the occasion when he covered a good portion of the Cheshire countryside with the contents of a farm septic tank that he had been called upon to dispose of.

SIX
FAMOUS PEOPLE
(WITH CHESHIRE CONNECTIONS)

Ian Botham

Mention Ian Botham to many Cheshire people and the local connection that comes to mind is not that he was born in Heswall, though he was, on November 24 1955. No, the image that often arises is that of "Beefy" in his 1980s hippy period, performing cricket feats at the Birtles Bowl.

A nation was thrilled and fascinated by the match at Headingly in 1981 when a Botham inspired England followed on and beat Australia; the fascination for watchers of the antics at the Birtles Bowl was somewhat different.

Here, on 10 acres of ground at the village of Birtles near Chelford, eccentric beatnik, disc jockey and general man about the pop scene, "Lord" Tim Hudson (a local lad, born in Prestbury) established a cricket ground with a pavilion painted in rainbow colours. But this was no mere venue for the trundlers and agricultural heavers of village cricket. Hudson became "Beefy's" manager for a time and persuaded, not only his main man, but the likes of Geoffrey Boycott and Viv Richards to turn out in the games he organised at his ground.

Botham adopted the offbeat dress of his new friend and the media lapped it up. Rock bands and flower power arrived in cricket.

As is often the case with the unorthodox, tears came fairly quickly, despite talk of the England star featuring in the lead role in the latest James Bond film. Botham and Hudson fell out spectacularly and eventually the Lord of the Manor of Birtles retreated to America.

A few years later he was back with his family, including daughter River Hudson, for a brief attempt at reviving the glories of the Birtles Bowl, but to no avail – the neighbours and the planning laws were against him – and again peace settled and the undergrowth grew.

Botham has admitted in recent years to his embarrassment over that period in his life. Fortunately it has not stopped him entertaining cricket fans with his television commentaries.

Leonard Cheshire

I did "meet" Leonard Cheshire once. I was walking through Shepherd Market in London and he was coming the other way. I looked at him and registered who it was, he looked at me, gave a pleasant, shy grin (no doubt hiding a resigned thought of, "heck, he's not going to stop me and want a chat is he?") and we continued in opposing directions.

Somebody once recounted to me the story of how in the 1950s they had been a junior officer on No 617 Squadron, of Dam Busters fame and Leonard Cheshire, former CO of the squadron as he was, had attended a dinner in the mess. My informant, being so junior, was placed well away from the top table and didn't have a clear view, but he later learned from the Commanding Officer of an oddity of Cheshire's appearance.

On greeting the honoured guest, the CO had been a bit puzzled about the gongs that Cheshire was parading. The Victoria Cross ribbon didn't seem to be present and neither did any representation of the Distinguished Service Order or the Distinguished Flying Cross. Yet before the CO was one of the greatest and most decorated Royal Air Force flyers of the Second World War.

A suspicion began to form in the CO's mind and gradually it became apparent what had happened. Rushing out of the house earlier in the day Cheshire had grabbed a set of ribbons to display in the evening. Later he realised that, by mistake, he had picked up the fruit salad belonging to his wife, Sue Ryder, charity founder herself and wartime member of the Special Operations Executive.

Because he was Cheshire this didn't bother him at all. Lesser men might complain if their MBE was omitted from some document, but not being able to advertise to the world, ownership of a VC, was of no consequence to this great man, who was linked to Cheshire not only by his name, but by his birth. He came into the world on September 7 1917 at the Egerton Nursing Home, Egerton Road, Hoole, though his early life was spent in Oxfordshire.

Both these stories illustrate the problems of trying to stereotype people. Geoffrey Leonard Cheshire gained a reckless and racy reputation at Merton College, Oxford, where his exploits included setting an undergraduate record for the fastest journey by car from Hyde Park Corner to Magdalen Bridge. Perhaps, in Shepherd Market, five minutes of walking time from Hyde Park Corner, my appearance had interrupted thoughts taking him back to his undergrad days.

He joined the Oxford University Air Squadron and moved on to a permanent commission in the RAF, serving as a bomber pilot, initially on the Armstrong Whitworth Whitley. Later he would drop from Group Captain to Wing Commander to take over 617 and he would be awarded the only VC of the Second World War for heroism over a number of years, rather than for one or more actions in a short period.

This was the man of action, yet he was also a deep thinker, writer and selfless and self sacrificing champion of those in need in the years after the war. And wearing the right medals didn't matter to him.

Lewis Carroll

Charles Lutwidge Dodgson was born in Daresbury on January 27 1832 and moved to Yorkshire 11 years later. He was at Rugby School, where the reputation of being "the most masculine school in England" has perhaps only been finally dispelled with the gradual admission of girls from 1975, reaching the daunting heights of the first head girl in 1995.

Alice's Adventures in Wonderland was published in 1865.

Mike Jones

The football referee who will have to live, for the rest of his career in football at least, with an image of a red beach ball. A Liverpool fan threw it on to the pitch and the distraction helped Sunderland get the real ball past the Liverpool custodian and into the net. Former Premier League referees, now earning a crust as pundits, queued up to draw attention to No

5 of the laws of football that, amongst other things, says that a referee, "stops, suspends or terminates the match because of outside interference of any kind."

Sir Adrian Boult

A schoolboy fan of Sir Henry Wood and later a revered conductor and Companion of Honour, he was born in Chester.

Trafford Leigh-Mallory and George Mallory

From Mobberley. Trafford was the leader of No 12 Group in the Battle of Britain in 1940 and did not impress many people nearly as much as Keith Park who led No 11 Group at the heart of the fighting. He had changed his name to Leigh-Mallory when his father did, but brother George did not follow suit. George was amongst those uninspired with Trafford, remarking that, "He affects magnificence, rushing about in a splendid Crossley car and giving orders with the curt assurance of an Alexander the Great, or Lord Northcliffe or Rockefeller."

Both brothers died young. Trafford in an air crash in 1944 and George on Everest with Andrew Irvine in 1924. They may have been the first to reach the summit, but we do not know.

Paula Radcliffe

Born in Daverham in a blizzard and went on to become a star of British athletics. Her very public comfort break during the 2005 London Marathon was later voted "Top Running Moment in History", which may make the likes of Roger Bannister (first sub four minute miler) pause to reflect on what it takes to achieve sporting immortality. No doubt many have now forgotten that Paula went on to win the race.

Ronald Pickup

Arrived in the world in Chester in 1940 and he's one of those actors who turns up everywhere including Dr Who, Waking the Dead, Dalziel and Pascoe, Long Day's Journey into Night. Crown Court and The Lion the Witch and the Wardrobe. He's played Albert Einstein, Edward Carson and Prince John in Ivanhoe too. In an episode of Bergerac he appeared as Sir Anthony Villiers, an exponent of the Sark Lark, a form of financial malpractice that no longer exists, now the Channel Islands have cleaned up their acts.

Joan Bakewell

Perhaps it's best not to mention what Frank Muir said about her, because Joan claims to hate being reminded of it. But Frank wanted to make the point that he thought she was both very intelligent and very attractive.

Joan, journalist and broadcaster, grew up in Hazel Grove.

George Rodger

Born in Hale in 1908, he photographed the Blitz, including the destruction wrought in Coventry and later the concentration camp at Bergen-Belsen. He is also remembered for recording everyday life in Africa.

Hewlett Johnson

"The Red Dean" of Canterbury was born in Manchester, but educated at Macclesfield Grammar School and was a vicar in Altrincham. He apparently saw no contradiction between his Christianity and his Communism

Henry Cotton

Golfer whose many achievements included increasing the status of the sport's professionals. He came into the world at Church Hulme, now better known as Holmes Chapel.

David Coleman

Yes, I know this sports commentator was highly knowledgeable, but his ability to see a triumph in a British athlete finishing 17th was wearing, though perhaps not as much as his constant "one-nil", "two-one", after a goal was scored at football. He was born in Alderley Edge and early in his career was a reporter on the Stockport Express.

There are other ways of looking at it. David Hemery won gold in the 400 metres at the 1968 Mexico City Olympics and his take on Coleman's commenting style was:-

"His voice actually engenders some of the adrenaline that people identify with, and he can create such a spirit of excitement that it helps people to live in the moment."

Though David Coleman was so famous for his less than intellectually convincing pronouncements that the column of such material in *Private Eye* was was named "Colemanballs", every journalist has done the same.

Graham McGarry, for instance, as Sports Editor of BBC Radio Stoke, was happy to own up to declaring on air, "The assistant manager of Crewe Alexandra, Neil Baker, has got his hands in his pockets and he's scratching his head wondering what's going on."

In passing, people from other parts of the country will not realise that despite Crewe Alexandra being in Cheshire and the Potteries teams, Stoke City and Port Vale, being in Staffordshire, they are all pretty close and a fair amount of rivalry exists. If I ever write a book on Staffs I'll explain how Port Vale got their name.

One of my slip ups did not see the light of publication, thanks to an alert secretary and Gill, if you are out there, thank you again.

I had the task of writing an obituary of a successful businessman who had died without warning in his mid-forties. This chap could turn round a failing business with a few deft touches, but his many and various skills did not include charm and what I suppose now must be called person management. In fact, the people who worked in proximity to him soon found that he was a tyrant.

Nevertheless, the chap had died young, had left a grieving family and had departed the businesses he ran better than when he found them, so it was natural in the obit to make some attempt to gloss over his most glaring faults, though not, for the sake of posterity and honesty, ignore them completely.

Struggling to deal with this situation, I wrote, "Mr X was a very down to earth person."

As I say, Gill saved the day.

Fred Perry

Stockport local hero. Perhaps another British player will have won a Grand Slam tennis tournament before this book comes out. The Fred Perry Way is a 14 mile long walking route in the Borough of Stockport, from Reddish to Woodford. There is a blue plaque on the house where he was born in Carrington Road, Stockport, but there seems to be some dispute as to whether it is the right house.

Stockport didn't wait too long to honour Fred Perry. He was made a Freeman of the Borough in 1934.

Kerry Katona

It's a bit difficult to think of much more of an insult than for Wikipedia to describe your profession as "media personality", but that's the fate of this former Atomic Kitten singer, based in Wilmslow and for some time the media filled much space recording the troubles in her life. But perhaps things have looked up. In the spring of 2010 she appeared on the cover of OK magazine.

Chris Evans

Really Cheshire can only claim the "love him or loathe him" DJ because he was born in Warrington, technically Cheshire now, but traditionally part of Lancashire.

If Warrington had stayed put Cheshire would have had to do without Chris Evans – what a thought that is!

Lady Hamilton

The village of Ness, near Neston was the birthplace of the girl, who after a complicated set of relationships and a considerable rise in the social scale, became Lady Hamilton and then the mistress of Lord Nelson.

Peter Butterworth

Now there's an actor that people of a certain age remember, from the Carry On films, from children's television and Dr Who. He was in an episode of Dad's Army and one of Dixon of Dock Green as well.

Peter was born in Bramhall in 1919 and died suddenly, aged 59, while waiting to go on stage in pantomime.

He's really part of a theatrical dynasty. He was married to Janet Brown of the Mrs Thatcher impersonations. His son, Tyler Butterworth, has appeared in any number of things including the Darling Buds of May, Bergerac, Last of the Summer Wine and Rumpole of the Bailey and Tyler's wife, Janet Dibley has a string of acting credits too.

Then there's the wonderful story – and Tyler assures me that it's what really happened – that follows on from the fact that Peter was a wartime naval officer, who became a prisoner of war and was a helper in the celebrated "Wooden Horse" escape. Vaulters exercised on the horse, men inside it dug a tunnel and others disposed of the soil by dropping it from bags in their trousers.

However, when the film The Wooden Horse was made, Peter went for an audition, omitted to mention his real life involvement and was turned down on the grounds that he didn't appear heroic or dashing enough.

On his gravestone, at Danehill, Sussex, are the words, "Life is real, death is the illusion".

Christopher Isherwood

He went on to acquire a cosmopolitan aura, but Christopher Isherwood was born in Cheshire and bred there too to some extent. He took his bow in 1904 at Wyberlegh Hall, High Lane, on the Marple Hall estate.

In a recent article in *Stockport Heritage* magazine, Erik Eriksson put the case for Isherwood's second novel, The Memorial, to receive more attention than it does. Its theme is, "the mutual destructiveness of the mother and son relationship ------ in the context of the First World War." The memorial referred to is that to the fallen of the war in All Saints' churchyard, Marple, on which appears the name of Isherwood's father, Edward Bradshaw-Isherwood.

The son – mentored by E M Forster and mentor to W H Auden - lived in Denmark, Germany and elsewhere, but he returned to Cheshire, despite having mixed feelings.

Eriksson quotes an Isherwood diary entry written in Cheshire:-

"This afternoon I walked to Ridge End ------ a wall of dark, mottled piled stones, a corn golden pony in a field scattered sparsely with snow and beyond New Mills smoke stacks rising so august and beautiful between the snowy hills. I felt deeply moved. This is my native country. Thank God for it – and thank God on my knees that I got out of it."

A character in The Memorial describes Stockport – "a dirty old hole of a place, but she'd liked it as they'd rattled over the setts. Of course it was different from the south; grey, smokier, barer than anything she'd seen in London –but she was determined to find some romance in it. And Mr Vernon had supplied that. 'They always say,' he told her, 'Stockport is like Rome – it's built on seven hills.'"

Stockport Heritage magazine, it should be said, deserves support. Kept going year after year by local journalist Steve Cliffe, always seeming on the brink of defeat or sale, it has not only recorded the history of the Stockport area, but has fought with success to save that history.

Sir Joseph Whitworth

Whitworth is a common name around Manchester and Sir Joseph added to its lustre. He was born in Stockport in 1803 and appears to have shown an early talent for working with machinery. His first wife Fanny was a Cheshire native too, the daughter of a bargemaster from Tarvin.

While working for Henry Maudslay in London, Whitworth found the procedure for creating a truly plane surface, so that for all kinds of sliding tools frictional resistance might be reduced to a minimum.

He later explained his first move, "was to abandon grinding for scraping. Taking two surfaces as accurate as the planing tool could make them, I coated one of them thinly with colouring matter and rubbed the other over it. Had the two surfaces been true the colouring matter would have spread itself uniformly over the upper one. It never did so, but appeared in spots and patches. These marked the eminences, which I removed with a scraping tool till the surfaces became gradually more coincident. But the coincidence of two surfaces would not prove them to be planes. If the one were concave and the other convex they might still coincide. I got over this difficulty by taking a third surface and adjusting it to both of the others. Were one of the latter concave and the other convex, the third plane could not coincide with both of them. By a series of comparisons and adjustments I made all three surfaces coincide, and then, and not before, knew that I had true planes."

It's claimed that this account gives less credit than was due to Maudslay, but Whitworth was clearly an engineer on the up.

Later he contributed to the calculating machine of Charles Babbage and, in 1833, came back to the north west, to Manchester, where he was possibly a little economical with the truth when he put up his plate as, "Joseph Whitworth tool-maker from London". His work would be highly commended at the Great Exhibition. He designed a measuring machine, that assured his fame, as well as a device for street cleaning. Whitworth became President of the Institution of Mechanical Engineers and the Whitworth rifle was another manifestation of his inventiveness. He was a Fellow of the Royal Society and was made a baronet.

The Whitworth building at the University of Manchester is one of the many tributes to him.

Benny Rothman

Born Bernard Rothman in Cheetham Hill, Manchester in 1911, he had many associations with Cheshire during a long life that ended in 2002. In retirement he tended his allotment in Timperley.

A passionate communist, trade unionist and man of the out-doors, Benny Rothman is best remembered as a leader of the Kinder Scout mass trespass in 1932, when 400 walkers sought to reach the peak of the Peak District against the wishes of the landowners. Fighting broke out with gamekeepers, there were injuries and a number of the trespassers, including Rothman, were arrested. The charges included riotous assembly. Eventually Rothman and four others served jail terms.

The mass trespass soon entered legend and so did Benny Rothman, but his account of the event and his part in it has been disputed, notably by Tom Stephenson, also looked up to by many as a high priest of the outdoors.

Peter Barkworth

The Telford's Change and The Power Game actor was born in Margate, Kent and grew up in Bramhall. He wrote a book on acting frequently consulted by those who want to.

SEVEN
PASSING TRAINS

Amongst the railways of Cheshire there was the Great Central and North Staffordshire Joint Railway, which to the ill informed probably sounds very impressive. This however, was not a railway with tentacles in all directions. Its other name was the Marple, Bollington and Macclesfield Railway and it stayed firmly in Cheshire through its journey of 25 minutes or so.

The line was very much a product of mid-Victorian railway politics involving the North Staffordshire Railway, the Manchester Sheffield and Lincolnshire (forerunner to the Great Central) and the powerful and masterful London and North Western Railway, that wanted to control railway access to Manchester. But the North Staffordshire eventually struck a deal with the LNWR, making the Marple line less important. A link to the collieries of Poynton helped, but this was still essentially a rural byway and it disappeared off the railway map years ago.

Today the Great Central and North Staffordshire Joint is a footpath and bridleway, known as the Middlewood Way. In the middle of a wood – and in the centre of nowhere – you can find the site of Middlewood station. Actually, it was Middlewood Upper, belonging to the GC & NS Jt and you can still catch a train from Middlewood Lower and go to Buxton, Stockport or Manchester on the metals of the former LNWR.

Small can be valuable. I recently found a dealer selling a considerable number of varied railway uniform buttons. If you collect such things and wanted to add to your collection one from the GC & NS Jt, you would have had to put your hand in your pocket to the extent of £45; much more than the cost of the buttons, offered by the same dealer, originating from much more distinguished railway concerns.

EIGHT
A COUNTRY SEAT

Is there anywhere else in the country where horses and the means of looking after them, form such a prominent part of the landscape than Cheshire?

Within comfortable walking distance of where I live are at least six stables, often right next door to each other. Girls – and there are some boys too – can take up the hobby at three or younger and very often it's with them for life. The expense is enormous and you, or anyone you can persuade to help, is tied to the job day in and out, but clearly, despite the thrill largely passing me by, many people find great enjoyment and relaxation and respite in being around horses.

To be fair to myself, I did try. When my daughter started having lessons, aged not very much, I had a couple too. It was not a success, even though the stables found a horse they considered strong enough to take me on board. I couldn't even understand how to grasp the reins in the correct fashion and so I quickly retired to the sidelines.

The expense is not merely acquiring the horse, feeding it and finding somewhere to keep it. Tack, insurance, vets, farriers, lessons, worming, show entry fees (if you go in for that kind of thing), transport to the shows, hunt fees, if you are into that, membership of The Pony Club – it goes on and on. I know, I've been there with my cheque book.

Consolations for the expense include the opportunity to learn a whole new phrase book of swear words, with most of the teachers being the ladies.

Cheshire incomers will find themselves in a world of four-legged animals whether they like it or not and they should learn how to cope. For one thing, horses and their riders will often be encountered on the road and cars really should slow down and give them plenty of space – and it has to be said that many do.

* * *

A hint that horses may be taking over the area came in a recent report in Horse and Hound where it was claimed that, "More riders could claim compensation from local councils who fail to maintain bridleways following a landmark case in Cheshire. "

It reported that Gaynor Goodall has won £12,000 damages from Tameside Metropolitan Borough Council after she was thrown off her horse on a bridleway near Stalybridge.

Tameside County Court decided that the council had been negligent after it failed to repair the bridleway that had allegedly deteriorated and become dangerous to riders. Horse and Hound continued,

"Mrs Goodall's solicitor, Inderjit Gill from Jacksons, specialist equine solicitors, said the case sets a precedent.

"Local authorities are obliged to maintain bridleways as part of their remit or may suffer further legal cases," he explained.

"The Council's defence was purely that they couldn't afford to maintain the bridleway because of the recession. We weren't saying the condition of the bridleway should be improved, just kept in a reasonable state, which it obviously wasn't."

Mrs Goodall, 42, was riding with her eight-year-old daughter along the Gallows Clough bridleway, near Stalybridge in the foothills of the Pennines, on 7 July 2007, when her horse fell, throwing her off."

The culprits were boulders that had been swept down the hillside by rain.

Tony Turner, founder of Tameside Bridleways Association, part of the West Pennine Bridleways Association, supported Mrs Goodall and was in court to back the claim.

"This is a beautiful route and a fabulous ride, but it is in very poor condition and has been for many years," he said.

"Most of the length of the bridleway is dangerous — it was just a matter of time before someone got seriously injured. Now maybe the council will start to work with us.

"Tameside Council declined to comment."

Mrs Goodall claimed that her arm had "literally snapped in two", which I assume is an exaggeration, but it still sounds pretty nasty.

And note, "specialist equine solicitor" – there's an illustration of the impact of horses on Cheshire.

* * *

Your children, as well as you, will mix with horsey people, so I've jotted down a few tips on the jargon, so that you can join in and not look too silly. These come not from an expert, but from someone who has spent many years on the fringes of the hobby, learning about it by constant repetition. Remember, this is a guide aimed not at somebody who really wants to know about horses, but at those who merely aspire to nodding and shaking the head and saying yes and no in the right places.

However – and being pretty serious for a moment - if you are tempted to take up riding, let's be clear that this is a dangerous pastime as Mrs Goodall found out.

The former Government drugs adviser, Professor David Nutt, compared the risk of riding with the risk of taking ecstasy. That may or may not be true, but dangerous it is. One member of my family landed in hospital with serious head injuries and she wasn't even on the horse at the time of the accident.

I recall seeing my daughter, taking part in a show jumping competition, sailing through the air over a fence with the horse standing to attention on the approach side and, on another occasion, she was thrown off and then trodden on. Fortunately she was unhurt both times.

On the latter occasion I got the blame. It was at the Romiley Young Farmers Show, a big event in these parts and across the field a traction engine let off steam and startled daughter's steed. As I'm a bit of a steam anorak, this, by definition, had to be my fault.

So, learn the safety rules, wear the right equipment and remember that it's a long way down from a big horse and in those few moments of panic when something goes wrong, the horse may well try to avoid you but perhaps won't succeed.

Here they are then - some terms to throw into the conversation when you are around horsey people and they might help you get some idea of the thrust of the conversation. It's not a comprehensive list of course and the definitions aren't too learned – they are aimed at the ignorant like me.

Bit: The part of the bridle that enables you to communicate with the horse.

Canter: A series of bounds. Known as the right or left canter, depending on which foreleg is leading.

Conformation: The build of a horse, the symmetrical arrangement of the different parts.

Colic: Stomach pain that might turn out to be a killer. Get the vet immediately.

Colt: An uncut male horse less than four years old.

Crossbreed: Combining two breeds to produce the characteristics of both in one horse.

Dressage: Training that develops the physique and ability of the horse in harmony.

Equitation: The skill of riding on a horse.

Farrier: Yes, it's the person who puts new shoes on a horse, but there's rather more to it than that, including the ability to advise on hoof health. There is a range of qualifications for today's farrier. So, not all medical work on horses is carried out by vets. There are also physiotherapists, chiropractors, dentists, "bonemen", horse whisperers, psychics and no doubt others as well.

Filly: A female horse that is less than four years old.

Gelding: A male horse that has been castrated.

Gymkhana: An organised meeting of horses and riders to take part in horseback activities – one of those words that the English language acquired from India, probably from the Hindi name for a racket court. In English it was applied to other sports , though you only hear it now in relation to horses.

Hands: The normal unit of measurement – one hand is the same as four inches.

Livery: The boarding of a horse at a yard. Owners may do the work themselves or you will hear them talking about full or part livery; some or all of the work is done for them – at a considerable price.

Lunging: Training a horse while it is on a line.

Mare: A female horse that is at least four years old.

Martingale: Intended to prevent a horse raising its head too far, it comes in running and standing types.

Menage: An area where horses are trained.

Near Side: The left side of the horse.

Parturition: Giving birth – it never seems to be used for humans now.

Piebald: Black and white colouring.

Pony: Generally a horse is at least 14.2 hands and a pony is not. It's far from as simple as that though, as there are other characteristics, such as ponies tending to be hardier, so you can meet a horse that is below the normal size and a pony that is above it.

Reins: The direct contact between the rider's hands and the horse's mouth.

Rein back: It doesn't normally mean "slow down" as I had assumed, but to direct the horse backwards.

Roached: A mane that has been cut short.

Rosettes: Most people know what a rosette is, but it took me a long time to realise that in Britain a red rosette normally signifies a winner, blue is for second, yellow for third, green for fourth, pink for fifth and purple for sixth.

Senior Horse: Any horse that is more than five years old

Seat: Get this wrong and you will incur the wrath of the instructor and then fall off if you don't listen to what you are told. It's the way you place yourself in the saddle. The use of balance and weight are central issues.

Skewbald: Any coat colour except black, combined with white.

Stallion: A mature horse, male and uncastrated.

Tack: All that expensive equipment that you need before you go out riding.

Tie-down : A strap that comes between the horses front legs and is attached to a band at the nose – thus the animal may only move its head by so much and is more in a position to obey commands through the bit.

Trot: I know what a trot looks like, but it's difficult to explain. "The diagonal legs must be raised from the ground simultaneously and be replaced on the ground together, making two hoofbeats," is one way of putting it.

Yearling: Any horse between one and two years old.

NINE
HAZEL GROVE

The difficulty of living in Hazel Grove is convincing people that it exists. It must be a street name, like it is in various other parts of the country. Things are not made easier by the fact that the next village up the A6 towards the hills is called High Lane.

Every few years Hazel Grove has its five minutes of fame as the name of an often marginal Parliamentary seat – though boundary chopping and changing means that a large chunk of the place called Hazel Grove is now not in the constituency and the Hazel Grove constituency contains bits of all sorts of other places.

However, this fleeting fame or notoriety doesn't seem to help people to remember the place for the four or five years between elections. Perhaps they would be more likely to re-member the previous name of Bullock Smithy.

In 1901 Councillor Robert Jopling Fletcher became the author of *A Short History of Hazel Grove*, and according to him the blame probably lies at the front door of Mr Thomas Ashworth, who lived in the impressive Torkington House, but didn't like having an address derived from a blacksmith called Robert Bullock.

Mr Ashworth caused a proclamation regarding a festival in 1835 to be titled, "Reviving the Proper Name, Hazel Grove".

Clearly he was a man of some determination and not one to let the truth stand in the way of a good story.

Councillor Fletcher tells us that, "...there is no record of any instance where the name had been previously used and sub-sequent inquiries point out that the name was an alteration of the name Hessel Grave... which was not in the village at all, but a considerable distance up High Lane."

The author does concede though that the area was notable for the hazel trees that abounded, giving some respectability to Mr Ashworth's social pretensions. Some sources also stress that a committee existed that was in favour of the change and it is claimed that 3000 people took part in a parade in 1836 to celebrate the new image. It wasn't until the Hazel Grove drainage area was established in 1887 that the name became official though.

Another twist in this confusing tale existed until recent years, in the shape of a stone at the, now demolished, Red Lion pub, that proclaimed, "The Village of Hazel Grove, 1796". This, we are told, was actually cut in 1836 by one Issac Broadhurst.

There were more jollifications, marking name change anniversaries, in 1886, 1936 and 1986.

Apparently anyone seeking the grave of Mr Hessel should search nearly opposite the Robin Hood pub on the outskirts of High Lane.

Actually, whatever the difficulties today of explaining to people where you live, it was worse in Councillor Fletcher's time. He gives the details of various parishes and township names that were still applied to parts of Hazel Grove.

For example, a contemporary photograph of part of the main street in his book has the caption (referring to two of the many pubs that still exist), "The Grapes (Norbury) and The Three Tuns (Bramhall). The House on the right-hand side is in Bosden." And this all in Hazel Grove "high street".

One of my favourite moments in "The Grove" came on June 21 1977. The Queen and Duke of Edinburgh were making their Silver Jubilee tour of the country and the Royal train set them down at the station for a day of visiting the Manchester area.

Early that morning I caught a train into Manchester. Perhaps it was not entirely surprising that people were beavering away, making the station look much more presentable than it normally did for commuters, but these things can go too far.

I swear this is true. They really were hiding the gents' toilet by placing shrubs in pots around it and outside on the low pavement, where the Royals would get into a car, a tiny ramp was being created, perhaps a couple of inches deep. It looked most odd and could have been of no assistance at all in stepping into the vehicle.

Naturally, no sooner had the distinguished visitors departed, than these extraordinary manifestations were removed.

So, it really is the case that the Queen doesn't know that railway stations have gents' loos.

TEN
FOOTBALL

Rather as the Thames divides London, and south London is a foreign country to those from over the river, so, in football terms at least, there is a south Manchester and a north Manchester. Some people support a lower division team, such as Stockport County, Bury or Rochdale, but other than that you usually find Manchester City fans in the south and United followers in the north.

I spotted this piece of relevant literature on the internet and it well illustrates the point:-

There was a girl from Stockport,
Her name was Hazel Grove,
She started supporting City,
When she was eight years old,
She's been to nearly every match,
She's only missed a few,
She's never seen them win a cup,
And now she's forty-two!

Sadly, there is truth in this, it has indeed been a long wait for glory amongst those who follow the blue shirts and red shirt followers are only too happy to remind all they meet of that fact.

By the way, one of Sky presenter Jeff Stelling favourite jokes (and part of his brilliance is that he can get away with frequent repetition of his favourites) also has much truth in it.

"There'll be dancing in the streets of Bournemouth tonight", he will say when a United shot hits the back of the net. When I've walked past the catering vans into Sir Matt Busby Way before a match at Old Trafford I've studied the coaches lined up with labels displaying which branch of the supporters club they have carried to the game. Bournemouth, Ross on Wye, Edinburgh, North Devon and so it goes on. No doubt some of the members are originally from Manchester, "The Rock 'n' Goal Capital of the World", as one supporters' club website puts it, but otherwise it seems a sad way to be a football follower.

However, I do know one chap, who claims to be a Sunderland supporter and grew up about as far away from Roker Park/the Stadium of Light as it's possible to get in the British Isles. His explanation is that when he was at school he wasn't much interested in football, but he thought he'd better choose a team, as most of the other lads had one. He was interested in aircraft, the Sunderland had been a famous flying boat and his lifetime allegiance was settled.

ELEVEN
SAY CHEESE!

A significant proportion of my early working life was spent in Ye Olde Cheshire Cheese – and the Printer's Devil, the Punch, the King and Keys and other pubs around the Fleet Street area of London EC4.

The great things about the Cheshire Cheese as a pub were the secret corners, the venerable atmosphere and, like those other pubs, the considerable newspaper characters that you might well bump into. And "Ye Olde" it is – pubs on the site date back at least to the 16th century and one of them burnt down in the great fire of 1666 – however, the cellars may have survived and may even take us back to a Carmelite monastery of the 1200s.

The fame of Cheshire cheese, as a magnificent product from one of Britain's great dairy areas, has spread well beyond London. There is a monument to its splendours in the town of Cheshire, Massachusetts.

TWELVE
WHAT'S IN STORE

It has spread everywhere, but the Co-op is seen as a bit of a northern institution and it is one that has come roaring back in the last few years. They might not own coal mines, build railway wagons or run libraries any more, but those green (in colour, and they would say in methods too) convenience stores have brought them right back into focus.

But there is a great Co-op myth, perpetuated by pub quiz setters across the land. It's a long way from the truth that the first Co-op store in the world was opened by the 28 "Rochdale Pioneers" in that (wash my mouth out) Lancashire town in 1844. The consumer co-op founded in 1769 by the Fenwick Weavers Society in Ayrshire was one early example of co-operation that many historians point to and there was even a Co-op Society in Rochdale, that failed, before the Pioneers came along.

Cheshire too could teach Rochdale a thing or two about co-operation. There is evidence that a predecessor of the Stockport Great Moor Co-operative Society was founded in 1831, although admittedly that evidence only consists of a fragment of the accounts. However, Cheshire can still beat Lancashire even if you don't count the fragment. It is clearly recorded that a meeting was held on May 26 1844 (that's seven months before they set up shop in Rochdale) to bring two organisations together in Great Moor to form one Co-operative Society.

Great Moor is an outer suburb on the south side of Stockport and today its Co-op Society forms part of the (almost) all embracing Co-operative Group, but for many years small societies tended to be fiercely independent. The centenary history of Stockport Great Moor records that, "In 1912 the Society were approached by the Stockport Co-operative Society with a view of considering the question of amalgamation and it was resolved that the question be not considered."

Old Co-op hands will know that it was many years before such questions were regularly and positively considered in co-operative boardrooms.

The same history records something that seems to demonstrate a degree of farsightedness on the part of the people of Great Moor. In 1915 the Society decided to insure its buildings and contents against hostile aircraft (and what those aircraft dropped?).

Other signs of the times are there in the records:-

"Owing to the scarcity of male labour, Mrs Sinker, Mrs Booth and Miss E Aspinall assisted in the serving of customers." Whether the three ladies had impact, good or bad, on sales is not recorded.

Then again, the decision was taken in 1916 to send a subscription to the Army Christmas pudding fund.

Strange isn't it, that very few people can grasp that the Co-op isn't one organisation with its headquarters in Manchester? With the rise of The Co-operative Group and merger after merger, that's a lot closer to the truth than it used to be. However, traditionally, there were thousands of retail Co-op

societies, often more than one to a town or village and all to-
tally independent of each other. Most of them were members
of the Co-operative Wholesale Society as it was called and
took many of their goods from it, but they controlled the CWS
and not the other way round.

I came across this blind spot a few years since in the
museum in the attractive town of Glossop, a little way across
the border and up in the Derbyshire hills.

The captions were wrong on this point on a series of
photographs of old Co-op buildings, but the local historian I
was directed to just would not have it and there was no answer
to my follow-up letter.

THIRTEEN
ROUTE CANAL

There was a time when the Co-op travel people would, every year, in the style of Frank Sinatra's retirements, advertise a "last chance" to sail on the Manchester Ship Canal. Perhaps they were within their rights to use a little bit of poetic licence because the Co-operative Wholesale Society had been a major force in the building of the canal, that begins its journey to Manchester at Eastham on the Wirral. It was a CWS-owned ship that was the first to traverse the canal in revenue earning service.

The existence of the canal enabled Manchester to become one of the country's major ports, despite being 40 miles from the sea. That's no longer the case, but the Ship Canal hasn't closed either and the Peel Ports Group that runs it today claims that it still carries 8 million tonnes of cargo a year.

FOURTEEN
A SOLID PLATFORM

Is there anywhere more readily associated with railways than Crewe? There are other British towns that grew mightily with the arrival of the great new form of transport and a railway works – Swindon, Eastleigh, Ashford and the Norfolk outpost of Melton Constable amongst them, but they don't seem to have entered into popular culture to the same extent.

The Grand Junction Railway came in 1837 and soon that became part of the London and North Western Railway. The LNWR works came to dominate the growing town and the railway's paternalistic approach led to such benefits as Queen's Park. In true Victorian fashion the LNWR expected everyone to know their place, but that place could be much more comfortable than the average if you worked for the LNWR.

The man who is remembered as a towering figure in both the LNWR and the life of Crewe is Francis William Webb (1836-1906) who became Locomotive Superintendent of the Railway in 1871. Shortly afterwards the title of the post was changed to Chief Mechanical Engineer.

Webb was an avid inventor and, more than 100 years after his death, the controversy over his standing as a railway engineer rumbles on amongst the more learned anoraks of the fraternity. He produced some successful standard classes, but his "compounds" (a form of locomotive in which steam is expanded in two stages) seem to have had fewer fans.

On the civic side, Webb was an alderman on both Crewe Town Council and Cheshire County Council and was twice mayor of the town.

He is usually represented as a formidable figure, so it takes some getting used to that Crewe has commemorated him with "Frank Webb Avenue". Perhaps intimates did address him as "Frank", but one suspects there weren't many of those and he doesn't look like a "Frank" in his pictures.

The LNWR was one of the largest of the railway companies before the railway grouping of 1923, but, even so, it is noteworthy that three of its employees won the Victoria Cross in the First World War.

Private Wilfred Wood of the Northumberland Fusiliers won his in Italy in 1918, when he knocked out two enemy machine gun posts on his own initiative and took 140 prisoners.

Private Ernest Sykes, also of the Northumberland Fusiliers, earned his award near Arras in France in 1917, when he brought back wounded men under fire and remained in the open attending to the wounds of others.

Lance Corporal "Jock" Christie of the London Regiment won the VC in Palestine hurling grenades at Turkish soldiers advancing in a trench.

All three men had locomotives of the LNWR Claughton class named after them, though this may have been a dubious honour as the class gave much trouble.

Perhaps it is remarkable that these three heroes survived the war. Indeed, in later years, there were it seems, occasions when one could ride in a train driven by Wilfred Woods, with Ernest Sykes as the guard.

Mr Woods, who lived much of his life in Hazel Grove, was apparently a man of contrasts. He had won the VC, then he survived as a foreman in the tough atmosphere of Longsight locomotive shed in Manchester, yet a railwayman who knew him described to me, "a quiet little man who wouldn't say boo to a goose." It's often the case, however, that those who do these deeds present a different face to the world on other occasions.

It was also decided to name one of the Claughton locomotives in memory of the LNWR war dead. In 1984 I had the great privilege of listening to a very elderly gentleman describe how the idea had been his and how he had supervised the project.

Kenneth Cantlie had been a premium apprentice, in the charge of the chief mechanical engineer of the railway, Charles Bowen Cooke and he had raised with his boss the notion of a memorial engine, though his proposal was that the name to be displayed should be "Victory". Bowen Cooke took the idea to the Board and it was approved, however with a change of name to "Patriot".

Colonel Cantlie, as he had become, explained to me that one unusual problem occurred during construction of the locomotive. It had been intended that it should carry the number 69 and plates had been cast, but somebody pointed out that this would make the railway a laughing stock amongst the returning troops as "soixante neuf" was a euphemism for Belgian brothels, apparently arising from the street number of one of them.

The locomotive was instead given the safer and appropriate number, 1914.

The LNWR became part of the London Midland and Scottish

Railway and a new class of locomotives was created, some members of which utilised parts from Claughtons. The Patriot name was transferred to the first member of the new class and the class became known as "Patriots".

Patriots also carried the names of Wilfred Woods and Ernest Sykes, but "Lance Corporal J A Christie VC" was discarded. This would seem to be because he had left railway service, which seems a bit hard.

Two other railway companies named locomotives in honour of the war dead. The Great Central Railway had "Valour" and the London Brighton and South Coast Railway, "Remembrance".

* * *

It could be argued that Crewe is the hallowed home of train spotting and that from there the number-recorders and rivet counters have spread around the world.

In steam days and even into the era of the diesel, there always seemed to be a crowd of spotters on the platform ends when I passed through. Why not, with so much entertainment to be had, lines shooting off in all directions and some of the most impressive locomotives of their day to be added to the collection?

Multiplying the fun was the fact that locomotives from a wide area would arrive and depart for attention at the Crewe works and, once the repairs were completed, "ex works" locomotives would do "running in turns", often hauling trains that would normally be considered well below their station in life. Frequently steam locomotives running in would haul local trains over the Crewe to Shrewsbury line through Whitchurch.

It helped that, between the wars, the big four railway companies were pioneers of public relations techniques. In the 1920s the Southern Railway, for instance, was facing much public criticism over such matters as late trains and dirty trains. So a journalist was hired from the Daily Express to improve the company's reputation. Eighty five years on, the trains are still dirty and late, but the man from the Express, John Elliot, did so much for the railway's reputation that he eventually became the line's acting general manager.

One of the techniques that all the big companies used was to name their locomotives, especially the big express passenger engines. Often these names were designed to conjure up romantic and patriotic thoughts, though the London and North Eastern Railway fell into the trap of favouring names of racehorses. This led to strapping express locomotives named Pretty Polly and Spearmint.

The LNER was also obsessed with the names of its bosses and their country piles, leading to some renaming of the streamlined A4 class "Pacifics". Thus Kestrel became Miles Beevor and Sea Eagle became Walter K Whigham.

Great Western Railway locos often reached Crewe and that railway was even more obsessed with buildings.

Its "Hall" class of mixed traffic locos eventually ran to 330 examples, all but one of which carried a "Hall" name. Things became pretty desperate, with edifices featuring including Lady Margaret Hall and Albert Hall. In the end the names spread far outside Great Western territory, with Mottram Hall being a Cheshire example. It was suggested that when the last of the class emerged from Swindon works, the name would be found to be That's All, as it happened this proved not to be the case.

Back to Crewe though, and the London Midland and Scottish Railway that ran the show there. The LMS was possibly less obsessive, though certainly romantic and patriotic.

Those Cheshire train spotters would have seen frequently the Royal Scot class on the main line bearing military names that included: Royal Scot • Cameronian • Lancashire Fusilier • Old Contemptibles • Lovat Scouts • The Green Howards • The King's Royal Rifle Corps • The Rifle Brigade • The Middlesex Regiment • Honourable Artillery Company • Civil Service Rifleman.

And, tacked on the end: • The Boy Scout • The Girl Guide • British Legion.

Naturally The Cheshire Regiment was there too.

* * *

The really impressive locomotives that snapped the spotters out of any lethargy that had developed were the Princess Coronations, some of which had originally been streamlined. Many of them were named after aristocratic ladies and others after cities, hence: Duchess of Norfolk • Duchess of Rutland • City of Salford • City of Stoke-on-Trent • City of Chester.

Sir William A Stanier FRS was in tribute to the designer of the class and seemed to have rather an impressive ring to it.

* * *

There was the earlier and much smaller, in terms of numbers, Princess Royal class in which Princess Margaret Rose showed how the usual name of the Queen's sister had changed over the years and in which I found Lady Patricia particularly intriguing. Now I know that Princess Patricia of Connaught was a granddaughter of Queen Victoria, who relinquished her place in the Royal hierarchy, when she married the Hon Alexander Ramsay, a naval officer and commoner. From then on she was Lady Patricia Ramsay. Her husband was not all that common, being a son of the Earl of Dalhousie and Lady Patricia's former style lived on in name of the Canadian army regiment, Princess Patricia's Canadian Light Infantry – she had lived in the country when her father, the Duke of Connaught, had been Governor General.

Finally in this ramble through the more glamorous end of train spotting, as practised at Crewe, there was the extensive and sometimes maligned Jubilee class, that tended to be used on slightly lesser turns.

After Silver Jubilee itself (that name marked 25 years on the throne for King George V) came outposts of the Dominions and Empire: Prince Edward Island • Birhar and Orissa • Falkland Islands •

Naval grandees included: • Sturdee • Jellicoe (the Southern Railway had decided not to put his name on a Lord Nelson class locomotive in the 1920s, because the debate on how far the Battle of Jutland was a triumph or not was still going on.) • Prince Rupert • Collingwood • Howard of Effingham.

And Royal Navy ships: Renown • Revenge • Dreadnought.

Oh and there were Jubilees with names carried by both stagecoaches and early locomotives, including: Sanspareil and Novelty.

* * *

Now one of the great pleasures of teenage trainspotting in the 1940s, 50s and 60s and well before that too, was actually getting into the engine sheds, getting up close to the locomotives and savouring them in all their mucky glory.

Even though Health and Safety had not been invented then this was a strictly forbidden activity, though there were those railwaymen who were prepared to turn a blind eye. Those who indulged in this hobby soon discovered that the trick at larger sheds (as every spy and journalist will tell you) was to look as though you belonged. A donkey jacket, a small rucksack slung over the shoulder (purportedly for sandwiches), some smears of coal dust across the face and a confident air usually enabled you to wander around for as long as you pleased. What was perhaps a little surprising was that books were published telling spotters how to find every depot in the country.

The one before me is The British Locomotive Shed Directory compiled and published in 1947 by R S Grimsley and does it bring back the memories. I'm delighted to find in connection with the entry for Plaistow engine shed in London there is the reference I remember from years later to walking along the Northern Outfall sewer.

Mr Grimsley (it has to be a "Mr" doesn't it?) begins his introduction by noting an advantage of the Second World War.

"The late war provided locomotive enthusiasts with much interest; engines from one system on loan to another, American engines at work in Great Britain, specialised locomotives built for the War Department ----" – he continues on this theme for some way further.

So the war was a good thing for train spotters. Later in a lengthy introduction, the author does address the possible accusation that he is encouraging children to trespass and place themselves in danger.

The book "IN NO WAY GIVES AUTHORITY TO ENTER THESE PLACES", he declares as part of a lengthy health warning as we would probably call it today.

There were two large locomotive depots in Crewe, North and South and one has simpler directions than the other:-

Crewe North 5A (the 5A is the "shedcode" indicating a locomotive's place of residence and normally screwed to the smokebox door).

"The shed is on the west side of the line at the north end of Crewe station. The yard is visible from the Warrington and Chester lines.

"A footbridge connects the north ends of the station platforms and an extension of this bridge leads to the shed.

"The road entrance to the shed is at the end of Station Street."

(That sounds to me like a pretty tough one to "bunk", that is get into illicitly.)

Crewe South 5B

"The shed is in the fork of the main and Shrewsbury lines south of the station. The yard is partially visible from both lines.

"Turn left outside the main entrance to the station. Turn first left into Gresty Road and continue into Gresty Lane. There is a gate on the left-hand side between the two railway over-bridges and a flight of steps just inside the gate. A cinder path leads from the top of these steps to the shed. Walking time 20 minutes."

As Mr Grimsley made clear, steam locomotive sheds were not exactly open to the public, though often official permits to visit could be obtained through the post. So sprang up locospotting clubs that took their, usually young, members all over the country to collect numbers and see steam in action and on shed.

The one I was a member of in London was run by a very pleasant and efficient man who never gave me or my parents any cause for concern, but did eventually appear in a Sunday newspaper for reasons connected with teenage boys rather than steam locomotives.

There was, though I never had any connection with it, what seemed like a giant amongst such organisations. This was called Northern Railfans and I have before me a copy of the June 1957 issue of the enthusiasts' magazine, Trains Illustrated, to remind me how considerable its tentacles were.

For a start, it was so big that it needed far larger classified advertisements than similar bodies and three leaders. How familiar their names and addresses still are. Mr Brown and Mr Smith (!) were divisional secretaries, the one living in Glen View Street, Cornholme, Todmorden, Lancashire and the other in Underwood Lane, Crewe, Cheshire. However, the President was Mr Hawley of Goostrey, Cheshire, somewhat up the road from Crewe.

Oh the delights that were available to the members. There was a trip from Crewe, organised by the President, to visit sheds in the west country from Taunton to Plymouth, party rate rail travel was on offer for that. Mr Smith was masterminding a coach trip from Crewe around the Welsh borders, while Mr Hawley was taking a coach party round the (railway) sights of Manchester. The fortitude that those men must have had.

And this is only a selection of what you could have access to for a subscription of two shillings every six months. There was also a one shilling entrance fee, but that was waived if you were already a signed-up member of the nationwide Ian Allan Locospotters Club.

What uncelebrated heroes these fellows were. I bet there are many in Cheshire and the northern counties, now in middle and old age, who look back with glistening eyes to days full of steam, coal and grease, courtesy of the Northern Railfans Club. And I bet that plenty of those veterans still have their books listing numbers, with those that had been "copped" underlined.

FIFTEEN

TOURIST TRAP

The body dedicated to making sure that people don't merely drive through Cheshire on the M6 and head off somewhere else seems to be Visit Chester and Cheshire.

Clearly winning a plain English award is not one of their priorities. I went to the home page of the website and learned that:

"We are the tourism management organisation for Cheshire and Warrington, growing the sub-region's visitor economy with the support of over 350 stakeholders from the public and private sector.

"We are one of five tourism boards in the Northwest; funded and supported by North West Regional Development Agency, three local authorities and private sector tourism stakeholders in Cheshire."

I didn't know that "Cheshire and Warrington" was a sub-region, in fact I'm not sure that I quite know what a sub-region is, but I'm glad they left Warrington out on a limb as it shouldn't really be in Cheshire at all.

More encouraging is the "visitor guide" that the organisation sent me. There's much there to put Cheshire on the tourist map. How about the Minerva Shrine Festival for instance? We are told that the Roman Goddess has a link to Chester through a stone carved shrine. You can see the annual ritual offerings performed by Deva Victrix Roman Tours, Chester's own Roman display team.

An event that sounds a bit too energetic for me is the Frodsham Festival of Walks, a series of 13 guided walks through the market town and the surrounding areas, incorporating the Sandstone Trail and long and short walks.

SIXTEEN

WHEREVER I LAY MY HAT

Places to live in, visit or pass by:

Altrincham

Having looked down on people who spell it "Altringham", I've now discovered that they have some right on their side. Even in Victorian times that was a spelling that was used. Before that it was Aldringeham, possibly meaning "Homestead of Ald-here's people". Very much a Manchester commuter town now and part of the Greater Manchester conurbation, but you can still find rural spots that keep alive the area's past as a centre of market gardening, aided by the arrival of the Bridgewater canal in 1765.

The grandly named Manchester South Junction and Altrin-cham Railway took commuters to the city and was electrified as early as 1931. Now most of it is part of Manchester's Metrolink light rail system.

Appleton Thorn

A village close to Warrington where the sandstone village hall, once a school, is at the centre of local life. It claimed the title of CAMRA national club of the year in 2008 and captured the regional title in 2006, 2007 and 2009. "The heart of your community – fine ales, good company" proclaims the sign.

At the time of William the Conqueror, the village (well probably hamlet then, though it officially covered a much bigger area than it does now) was called Epeltune, meaning "the tun where the apples grew".

There's a story to the village hall. Locals got together in 1978 to save the crumbling building and turn it into a community centre. They persuaded the nearby Arley Estate to sell them the building. Funds were raised in all kinds of ways, including an excellent publication the *Thorn Tree Cook Book*. The rising thermometer telling the world how much cash had been raised is still fondly remembered and success was achieved.

Why Thorn Tree? We are informed that Adam de Dutton, a Norman, in the 12th century, planted in the area an offshoot of the Glastonbury thorn, said to have been grown from the staff of St Joseph of Arimathea.

Each June today the "Bawming the Thorn" ceremony takes place in the village. The current version of the event dates from the 19th century and involves children walking through the village and (now at the village hall) holding sports and games. The thorn tree is decorated, the children dance around it and sing a "bawming" song.

The cookbook from 1980 offered plenty of ideas for good things to eat, but there were also lots of handy tips.

Do you know how to revive a drooping lettuce? Wash it clean then place some coal in the rinsing water and leave for about an hour. And chips will be crisper and more evenly cooked if soaked for at least 30 minutes in cold water, drained and dried before cooking.

Fruit crumble can be improved by adding a dessertspoonful of quick porridge oats to the mixture. This makes it crisper and brings out the flavour.

After putting the jam in jam tarts, place one drop of cold water onto the jam and it will not then boil over.

Perhaps most useful of all, did you know that onions, when kept in the salad container of the fridge, will not make your eyes water when slicing?

I found my copy of this indispensable book among the thousands of secondhand volumes on offer at Cheshire Books, outside Frodsham and with the bonus of an excellent view across the countryside.

Bollington

A small hill town near Macclesfield and right on the edge of the Peak District. Today the possessor of an informative, if seemingly hyperactive, website. Or perhaps the website merely reflects a hyperactive town. The Civic Society "has never been more active", the Bollington Carbon Revolution is doing its bit to save the planet, the Discovery Centre continues to be very popular, The Brass Band, the Light Opera Group, the Festival Players "and so many other gifted groups" are on hand to stop residents having to sit at home at night and watch TV.

Slow down chaps: take time to look at all that super scenery. And how about getting rid of some of those exclamation marks?

One thing that people do travel to Bollington for, from far and wide is... the fish and chips. The Plaice serves them and does so very well.

Cheadle Hulme

Rather strangely, the home of Manchester Rugby Club (but then Stockport Rugby Club is in Bramhall). Otherwise effectively a smart Stockport suburb and Manchester commuter district, where well off men in trade built their "villas" from the 1850s and property tycoons soon pounced on the available land.

Chelford

To Cheshire people "Chelford" means "cattle market" and the market has been a feature of the village for 90 years and more. The railway disaster of 1894 causing the deaths of 14 people is no longer the definer of the village name that it probably once was. The accident was a freak event, involving a wagon caught by the wind during shunting. One of the locomotives hauling the train that came to grief was of the London and North Western Railway "Experiment" class. This may have been the occasion therefore when, so it has been claimed, the LNWR was slammed in a newspaper report for using an experimental locomotive on a passenger train. With such recklessness, disaster was inevitable was the theme.

Now there is excitement in Chelford because a local writer, Elizabeth Horrocks, has published her first novel and what a view of Chelford and the surrounding Cheshire countryside it presents.

This time travel fantasy starts in the present at Mid-Cheshire College (head office, Hartford, near Northwich), which is probably original in itself, but King Arthur and the legends surrounding Alderley Edge come into the plot. Chelford railway station appears in 1900, so do other features of the local land-scape and other periods of history. It's called The Edge of Doom.

Cholmondeley
(don't forget to pronounce it "Chumley")

Situated in the west of the county, between Tarporley and Nantwich and takes its name from the family that has been around since Norman times, though the present castle was brand new in the 19th century.

They go in for motoring at the castle and the annual Pageant of Power finds itself referred to as "The Goodwood of the North". A three mile circuit has been laid out in the grounds so that cars and bikes can put on a spectacular show for enthusiasts.

Combermere

Combermere Abbey and mere are in Cheshire – just. The Shropshire border runs through the park. Visible for a long way across the fields is the obelisk erected in 1890 to commemo-rate Field Marshal Viscount Combermere, who, despite the rank he reached was, we learn, considered "a damned fool" by Wellington, not always the most generous of critics. It is true that Stapleton Stapleton-Cotton, as he was then, was not called upon to assume a command at Waterloo, a source of great disappointment to him, but he did besiege and take the fort at Bharatpur (or Bhurtpore) in India, during a highly successful career – and he did name his son and heir, Wellington Henry.

The Abbey was founded in the 12th century and the "modern" house came along in the early 18th. Today it operates as an organic dairy farm.

Congleton

They did away with the Borough of Congleton in 2009 and now it's part of "East Cheshire", whatever that is. The town is underneath The Cloud, an outcrop of rocks, though if you just drive through on the A34 the main thing you will probably remember is the Tesco superstore and its enormous car park. Home to Ann Packer (now Brightwell) who seemed to burst from nowhere to win the women's 800 metres at the Tokyo Olympic Games of 1964.

Hack Green

As oxymorons go, the brown tourist signs around Nantwich pointing to the Secret Bunker must rate as Olympic class. Secret as it might have been once, it certainly isn't now.

Hack Green is the name of the "secret place" and it's a pretty rural area. Here during the Second World War a decoy site was established to attract bombs intended for the railway yards of Crewe, though given the frequent inability of the Luftwaffe at that time to find the location they were actually looking for, a raid on Hack Green might well have hit Crewe by mistake.

The decoy was replaced by a radar station. After years of dereliction part of the site was developed as one of the regional headquarters from which government would be carried on if nuclear war came our way. It didn't, the Home Office sold the site and it was privately opened as a museum in 1998.

Heswall

This town on the Wirral is "One of the UK's most sought after residential areas" according to its website. The "top" village is the commercial bit and the "bottom" village is the pretty bit, indeed it's a conservation area.

"The seeds of Heswall were sown when the Merchant Princes set up houses on the Wirral banks of the River Dee, initially as holiday retreats because of the spectacular views of Wales, wonderful scenery and invigorating fresh air." Clearly modern Heswall is determined not to be knowingly undersold.

Hyde

I wonder how many compilers of those pub quiz questions have defamed Hyde United FC over the years. It wasn't the present club that entered every football record book, by losing 26-0 to Preston North End in an FA Cup match in 1887. Instead it was a predecessor, Hyde FC (they folded during the First World War) that suffered that awful defeat. PNE were pretty good in those days, but I wonder if the Hyde manager survived.

Amongst footballers to come from Hyde was Warren Bradley, loaned by the amateur club, Bishop Auckland to Manchester United after the Munich air crash. He later signed for United. Bradley was that impossibility today, an England international, both as an amateur and as a professional. Amateur international games ceased many years ago.

Jodrell Bank

Now it's well over 50 years since strange structures appeared on the site of the University of Manchester's botanical station near Goostrey and people started to gawp across the fields, from the railway and from nearby grandstands such as Alderley Edge. So Jodrell Bank changed very quickly from being an extremely obscure place to a world famous location for radio astronomy.

That's what it remains today, despite funding scares. It is claimed that the first name of the founder, Bernard Lovell was borrowed for another famous, if fictional, scientist, Bernard Quatermass, whose adventures have caused many BBC watchers to hide behind the sofa over the years.

Knutsford

Retains a pleasant high street, from which most of the traffic keeps away and legal parking is perfectly possible with a little thought and willingness to walk a few extra yards.

Knutsford has achieved some additional fame with the recent television production of Cranford, the novel by Mrs Gaskell, loosely based on the town. It wasn't thought that modern Knutsford was olde worlde enough for the TV cameras. Lacock in Wiltshire was preferred, which is well used to TV and is more than pretty enough, as long as you ignore the nearby and enormous electricity pylons.

In 18th century Cheshire, health and safety executives and accountants marched alongside each other to run the show, just as they do today. The evidence can be found in the proceedings of the gentlemen who oversaw the building of Knutsford Church.

An entry for January 25 1747 reads, "It is unanimously agreed and ordered by the said commissioners that the metal of the present ffour bells belonging to the said parish be cast into a peal of ffive bells in case the steeple of the said parish church shall in the judgement of experienced workmen be thought sufficient to bear them and if not that such reduction shall be made in the mettall or weight of the new bells, as shall be thought proper and in such case that the best allowance which can be had be got for the overplus of the metal of the old bells and that the money arising therefrom be applied to-wards the expenses of casting the new bells."

The activities of the accountants at least can also be seen in Knutsford in the sense that this large and thriving town no longer has an office of its own local paper, the Knutsford Guardian. A reporter based in Northwich is now the means by which Knutsford folk learn what is going on through their best known "local rag".

More cheerfully, each year Knutsford keeps grand old English tradition alive by having a May Day celebration, including a personal appearance by Jack in the Green. He dates back several hundred years and turns up in various places around the country; originally flowers and leaves were collected and somehow chimney sweeps got in on the act, so the character of Jack was created. The concept waned, but has been coming back steadily over the past 30 years as a way of celebrating spring and attracting the tourists.

Macclesfield

"Maclesfeld" in the Domesday Book, then "Makelesfeld". It was "Maxfield" in every day speech to less distant generations (so somebody who lived there was a "Maxoinian") and "Macc" in today's parlance. All those words beginning with M may signify "Michael's Field", as in St Michael's Church. Though there is at least one other theory. The town became a borough in 1261 and perhaps before that.

Macclesfield is where Cheshire heads for the hills and where silk was at one time a considerable industry.

Buried in the town's cemetery is Sergeant Eric Bann, forced to bale out of a Hurricane over the Isle of Wight during the Battle of Britain and killed when his parachute failed to open. Eric came from a Macclesfield family who ran an agricultural machinery business and his letters to his parents in 1940 and his status as a fighter pilot made him a local celebrity.

Around a month before he was killed Eric wrote home from the airfield at St Eval in Cornwall, where his squadron was temporally based. He told his parents that his wife May was coming to Cornwall and he had been given leave to be with her.

He went on, "I read in the local Macclesfield paper that soon the seventeenth Spitfire will soon be given to the nation. Bravo Macc! All the boys of the RAF at this grand town. How I wish that I could be the lucky local boy to fly the plane."

Eric took a link with Macclesfield into battle. His mother had presented locally made yellow silk scarves to him and his comrades in No 238 Squadron's yellow section, Sergeant "Tony" Marsh and Sergeant Gordon Batt. Tony Marsh was also lost in the Battle of Britain, but Gordon Batt survived the war and still had his scarf when he died a few years ago.

A much more recent loss to be felt keenly in Macc was that of Keith Alexander, the manager of the town's football team, who died suddenly early in 2010.

Alexander was (with Lincoln City) the first black manager in English senior football. He seems to have presided with a sense of humour over Macclesfield Town's Spartan Moss Rose ground, set attractively nonetheless against a backdrop of the hills. On one occasion his complaints to a referee over a decision went too far and Alexander was banished from the touchline. At half time the official relented and allowed the manager back "as long as he remained inconspicuous".

Keith Alexander was heard to remark that for a 6ft 5in black man to remain inconspicuous in Macclesfield would be a considerable feat.

Macclesfield has a fun competition to find the best new building in the town – they see it as a means of demonstrating that they are not stuffy around there. In 2010 finalists included a take away, a boundary wall, a restored towpath, a budget hotel, a shop that sells and repairs false teeth and an Indian restaurant. One year chewing gum bins stormed to the title.

Marple

As with many of the towns and villages to the south of Manchester, Marple has moved from "industrial" to middle class commuter.

The industrial bit came mainly from Samuel Oldknow, born a Lancastrian, who established a weaving business in Stockport and Heaton Mersey and after this ran into trouble he arrived in Marple and nearby Mellor – across the Derbyshire border. The building of Mellor Mill began in 1790, three years after Oldknow came to the district – not content with mills, he built roads and bridges, established coal mines and constructed houses for his workers. The energy was remarkable and the transformation of a rural area was enormous.

Writing in Memories of Marple in 1899, Joel Wainwright, said of Oldknow:-

"To his liberal spirit the community in general was much indebted, but more especially was Marple which, at the time he removed from Stockport, was thinly populated and without any manufactures or anything but agriculture and that of an indifferent kind.

"He was one of the most zealous promoters of the Peak Forest Canal and of the turnpike road leading from Stockport through Marple to New Mills and Whaley Bridge, by means whereof a direct and easy land and water communication was obtained to all parts of the kingdom.

"Before his time that capital road (called New Road to this day) from Norbury Smithy through Marple to Strines and New Mills did not exist and Samuel Oldknow was its chief promoter. Prior to that period the main road was that known as 'Church Lane', leading behind the National Schools over the Brick Bridge, and so on down by Goytcliffe Torr, much of which is today obliterated, except to those who care to trace it out.

"He sank several coal shafts, built the corn mill, still used as a mineral mill, and built and worked the lime-kilns. The lime was first sent down to the low level of the canal by a tramway which he made, and of which traces still exist. He was in all ways a most pushing man, and was very anxious indeed to be able to say that he had sent the first boat load of lime down the new locks, and he was afraid that his arm of the canal from the lime-kilns would not be ready as soon as the locks above.

"His bridge near the Navigation Inn was the last bit necessary to finish his part, and he completed it in 1804, as the date of the bridge shows. So anxious was he to be the first, that he encouraged his men to make extra exertions by giving them ale posset every morning for breakfast, and so the bridge got the name of 'Posset Bridge', which it retains to this day. He won the day, as he deserved to do; his new boat properly named the 'Perseverance' gaining the prize."

Oldknow was a close associate of Richard Arkwright and borrowed much money from him.

Marple Bridge, just down the hill, is a pleasant spot, where the residents often like to think of themselves as separate to Marple. It's a place to live that must offer some cachet, as at the other end of the village Marple Bridge addresses evidently extend some way past the boundary with more rural Mellor.

The same phenomenon exists a little way away, where if you look at people's letterheads, Disley now appears to have claimed a good chunk of next door High Lane.

Mobberley

Good address, sprawls a bit. Some might regard Manchester Airport as conveniently close, others might see it as too close for comfort.

New Brighton

New Brighton seems a rather sad place and even the lady who runs a local website and says she loves it, has to admit that, "it is a shadow of its former self". She also points out that only the River Mersey separates the town from Liverpool, though it is not clear whether that is considered a GOOD THING or a BAD THING.

But, there is scope for looking back and remembering the good old days when the New Brighton Tower, design based on the Eiffel Tower, attracted half a million people a year. The Cheshire version was 544 ft high and boasted Winter Gardens, Assembly Hall and a cycle track.

From the top (and there were four lifts to take you there) you could see, so it is said, the Isle of Man, the Great Orme at Llandudno, the Lake District and the mountains of Wales.

Even those who stepped out of line were generously catered for. The Tower gardens had their own police force.

Things began to go wrong with the First World War and partial closure. Deterioration set in and some demolition took place. The remains were destroyed by fire in 1969.

Now there is a housing estate on the site and there's a park and football pitch too as reminders of happier days.

Northwich

At the meeting place of the rivers Dane and Weaver, famous for salt, but also for subsidence. Writing in the early years of the last century T A Coward described industrial dereliction in the town and went on:

"Yet Northwich is a busy thriving place. Half of the dilapidation is not due to poverty but to the difficulty of keeping buildings upright, for the ground beneath the whole district is unstable. As a matter of fact the condition of the town is not nearly so bad as it was; sad experience has caused property owners to seek means of holding houses together, with the result that half-timbering is brought up to date.

"All modern built houses in and around Northwich are more than half-timbered, they are frame houses, the timber framework holding bricks and mortar together. When the land sinks, as it frequently does, the house in toto is raised, and fresh foundations are put underneath; in many places the roadway itself has been raised again and again.

"The older houses exhibit cracks and ghastly wounds, frequently filled in with new bricks and mortar, while irons bolts and bars hold the unsteady tenements together. In some streets the windows and doors are a study, being devoid of right angles; a doorway, an irregular parallelogram, leans to the right, while the window next it, an inebriated rhomboid, falls gracefully towards the left. Parallel and equal-angled are not terms applicable to Northwich."

Happily I can report that the situation has improved. Worried about creating alarm and despondency by quoting this passage, I rang the office of Coulby Conduct, estate agent, in Northwich and was assured that subsidence is rarely a problem for house buyers now.

To cover all eventualities today's solicitors conduct a "brine search", along with all the more usual searches, when advising clients buying houses in and around the town.

Parkgate

A Village in the Wirral and on the River Dee, offering the chance to study marsh birds. Distinctive is the black and white main building of Mostyn House School and this independent, co-educational school, taking pupils from three to 18 (and the nursery deals with those from six weeks to five years) is a most unusual learning establishment.

It was founded in 1854 in Tarvin, by the Reverend Edward Price, and he quickly moved the school to Parkgate. In 1862 Mr Price re-located to Berkshire to establish another school and his nephew, A S Grenfell took charge at Mostyn House. There was a brief spell in the 1880s when a former pupil was Head, but otherwise, the Grenfells have been running the show ever since. Today, the headmistress, Suzi Grenfell, represents the sixth generation of the family to lead the affairs of the school.

Possibly the most famous of these Grenfells was Sir Wilfred (1865-1940), the son of A S, who was born at the school and was a pupil there. Afterwards he worked as a medical missionary in Newfoundland and Labrador, becoming a much loved and respected figure and the subject of at least one New-foundland stamp.

Rainow
(once it was called Ravenowe)

Right up in the hills, a lovely spot, but commuting must occasionally be a problem when winter sets in. Seek out a remarkably up to date village website, announcing lots of forthcoming Women's Institute activity.

Stalybridge

A cotton town, much re-vitalised, where a bridge was built that enabled the residents of Stayley Manor, and others, to cross the River Tame and thereby comes the name. The Stalybridge Brass Band claims to be the oldest in the world.

Stalybridge Celtic, the football team, keeps going and achieves success from time to time, though its glory days in the Football League are now almost 90 years ago.

Stanlow

Today "Stanlow" only conjures up "oil refinery". A very useful place that can look frightful or, in the dark and well illuminated, rather magnificent. However, things were, of course, different before industrialisation began in the 1920s.

Stanlow Abbey was founded in 1178 for the Cistercians, though even then opinion was that the scenery was dreary, the consolation being that the marshes round about provided them with groaning tables of fish and wild fowl.

Stockport

One thing Stockport is famous for (and proud of) is the railway viaduct carrying the London to Manchester main line. What many people don't realise (unless they have stood immediately underneath it) is that it is really two viaducts. Originally there were two tracks and then four were needed, so the second structure arose immediately beside the first.

Less famous are the viaduct's (and the town's) associations with artist L S Lowry and the River Mersey.

The Mersey flows through Stockport (without being the impressive sight that it is at Liverpool) and indeed it flows under the Merseyway shopping centre. So it is the Mersey Valley that needed to be bridged when the viaduct was built.

L S Lowry often contemplated and painted the viaduct and the Mersey underneath. He is mostly associated with Manchester and Salford and it is Salford Art Gallery that has a large collection of his work today, Lowry lived in Cheshire from 1948 until his death in 1976. Only just though – the forbidding house was situated in Mottram in Longdendale.

Perhaps less proudly advertised is a legal figure born in Stockport. Judge John Bradshaw (baptised 1602, died 1659) is described, baldly, by the Dictionary of National Biography as "lawyer, politician and regicide". Bradshaw was Mayor of Congleton and became a wheeler dealer in political and legal circles in London.

Then on January 10 1649 came the moment on which his fame, or notoriety, according to your point of view, rests. Bradshaw was appointed Lord President of the High Court of Justice set up to try King Charles I. Eventually , therefore, it was he who handed down the sentence of death on the Monarch. He died before the restoration, but revenge was still taken in grisly form. He was exhumed and hanged in his coffin at Tyburn, together with Cromwell and Ireton and their heads were later exhibited in Westminster Hall, where the trial of the King had taken place.

One may still see today Westminster Hall, where Bradshaw achieved his place in history and where many other moments of historic national importance have occurred. When the

House of Commons burnt in 1834 and again in 1941 (on that occasion caused by German bombs) the Hall was saved rather than the Commons chamber. Go in through the St Stephen's entrance to the Commons, as many visitors do and there immediately on your left is the scene of Judge Bradshaw's "glory".

There's another Stockport landmark not to be missed, in the form of the Town Hall. Manchester itself and most of the towns round and about wanted town halls that demonstrated civic pride and local wealth and Stockport's building on the A6 is up there with the best of them and can hardly be missed by a visitor to the town.

It was in 1908 that the then Prince of Wales came along to declare the building open. It was constructed in white limestone with a tiered clock tower, so for the last century and a bit it has often been referred to as "the wedding cake". Whether they held regular tea dances in the reign of King Edward VII I am not sure, but they do now.

Tarporley

"God's own country" according to a somewhat unoriginal former resident, but he has a considerable point. There's plenty of charm here, set amid some of the best of the countryside of the Cheshire Plain – unspectacular and extremely attractive at the same time. They prosper in Tarporley and one of the reasons is possibly the Tarporley Business Alliance that sets out to promote the village and commerce in the area. Be warned though, its website is not safe territory for those whose blood pressure rises at the misuse of apostrophes.

The Rotary Club and Round Table come together to organise the annual Tarporley carnival.

Tarvin

A village east of Chester. There has been a church on the site of the present St Andrew's since the 1100s. Much of the current building is from the 14th and 15th centuries. Presumably the usual 19th century alterations didn't ruin the place, because it is grade 1 listed.

Wrenbury

Wrenbury is right in the south of the county near the Shropshire border and surely in the top 10 of Cheshire's charming villages. Down by the canal, the Dusty Miller serves excellent food.

The last time I ate at the Dusty Miller I had to speak at the annual dinner of the Wrenbury and District branch of the Royal British Legion – there were 80 people packed in, not bad for such a rural area, though ladies didn't seem to be amongst those present. Perhaps news of the shape of the modern armed forces has not reached here yet.

Buried in St Margaret's churchyard (although the date on the gravestone is incorrect) is Sergeant Fred Eley a local lad who was a Spitfire pilot, lost in action in the Battle of Britain. His name appears at least four times around the church – on the gravestone, on a stained glass window remembering the parish fallen of the Second World War, in a book of remembrance underneath the window and on the war memorial in the churchyard.

Fred Eley's operational career in the RAF lasted five and a half months, which was considerably longer than some of his comrades in 1940. He had been a bank clerk before the war and a member of the Royal Air Force Volunteer Reserve.

Another local pub, the The Bhurtpore Arms in Aston, displays a letter that Fred wrote to his girlfriend on October 11 1939, from the sergeants' mess at RAF Tern Hill in Shropshire, where he was training.

Dear Molly

I expect you were wondering what had happened to me as I have been so long in writing. Believe me, there is little time left when we have finished work here. We fly till it is going dark and in the evening we have to swot. The amazing thing is that we all take it in the right spirit, and although it is a bit tiring we usually find plenty to laugh at. Anyway, it is all for our own good.

The flying side of the business is really good. That, we all enjoy. It is not unusual to do five hours in the air in a day. At that rate you can guess we are beginning to feel quite at home in an aeroplane. Once you get the hang of the new machines we have to fly it is quite simple. I have been flying solo for practically three weeks now. By that time one can make the machines do as one likes. A loop becomes just an ordinary thing, the thrill leaves it after a time.

We shall be here probably for another eight weeks – after which we go to a training camp somewhere in Scotland for another three weeks. It seems hard to believe there is a war on.

At first we had Sundays off, but that has been stopped now.

Bad weather has held up flying on one or two days and we have to make up the lost time somehow.

We are all keeping very fit. The food is still being kept up to scratch; in fact it is better than we had dared to hope for. Are you having any difficulty in getting such things as bacon and sugar?

The petrol rationing is a bit of a blow. Amongst the crowd who come from Stoke, several have cars, which did good work in getting us back to civilisation before the rations came in, but now they are all idle. It seems such a farce to think that one can't get hold of a drop of juice for pleasure, when I alone have used between 800 and 900 gallons since I have been here.

They reckon it costs £100 a week each to train pupil pilots, and I for one can well believe it. The expense of running a show like this is terrific. For every pilot there are nine men working on the ground. It seems incredible, but it is true.

Enclosed is a cheque for £1 5/- which is to repay what I owed you. You can cash it at the shop, or if you prefer, you can use it as a note.

I've very nearly forgotten what banking is like. I had a letter from the Burslem branch manager the other day, wishing me all the best of luck. They tell me that they will be very glad to see me back again. At the moment they have a new girl in my place, and if what they say is true, she's pretty hopeless as regards work.

Well, I must close now. It is getting late and we have to rise early.

Love to all

Fred

SEVENTEEN

CHESHIRE AND THE 45

Interested in Bonnie Prince Charlie and the "45"? For Cheshire people there's no need to journey north to the battlefield of Culloden, or the statue of Flora MacDonald outside Inverness Castle to walk in the footsteps of the Young Pretender. And there's certainly no need to go to the clansmen's monument at Glenfinnan, which, it is now claimed, wasn't built where the Jacobite standard was raised at all.

No, the Prince and his Army came our way on the march towards London and on the return journey, when, disagreeing with the decision to turn back, many of the men seem to have been in a worse mood than when they first passed by.

On the optimistic journey south the rebel army left Manchester and crossed the River Mersey in two places, one column a little below Stockport and the other, with the artillery and baggage, near Cheadle. The Stockport column was greeted by some Cheshire gentry and also by an old lady called Mrs Skyring, who was clearly a supporter of some passion, presenting the Prince with a purse containing money raised by selling her jewels, her plate and her trinkets.

Mrs Skyring is one of the less remembered tragic figures of the rebellion. When the decision of the Prince to retreat from Swarkestone, nine miles to the south of Derby, towards Scotland reached her ears, she is reported to have died, presumably from the shock of giving up her treasured possessions to a lost cause.

Marching via Woodford and Prestbury, the army reached Macclesfield, where the town and its people remained silent until four men were persuaded to ring a peal of bells and managed to do it backwards in the panic and confusion of the moment. Under duress, the mayor proclaimed his support for the Prince.

This gentleman learned his lesson. When news arrived in the town that the soldiers were returning, he and many of the gentry fled.

On the return to Stockport, it was discovered that a horse had been stolen – a threat to burn the town was made, but was not carried out.

This was not the first time that an army had passed this way, however, on one previous occasion the consequences were rather more serious.

This takes us back to the Harrying of the North by William the Conqueror in 1070 and there is a theory that his forces crossed the Pennines, passed through Stockport and sacked what is now Macclesfield and surrounding villages before three columns were formed to cross the county to Chester.

EIGHTEEN

BACK ON THE MAP

The winter of 2009/10 may have been, for many people, the worst for 30 years, but it made Cheshire feel loved and wanted.

All that salt that was needed and did or didn't arrive in the right place at the right time; most of it came from Cheshire. All those early morning shots of shivering reporters and lorries moving off into the darkness on their mission of keeping the country moving. Wonderful publicity it was for our county.

At Winsford, for instance, Salt Union runs what is claimed to be the UK's biggest rock salt mine. Somehow though those shivering reporters must have got it all wrong. So forget the supply shortages and the disputes between salt suppliers and local authorities.

It says on the Salt Union website that, "The company produces salt year round, building stock levels through the spring, summer and autumn, for use by governments and local authorities during the winter months."

The statement carries on, "The company works in partnership with local authorities and private contractors across Britain, to find practical solutions for the local supply, safe storage and spreading of rock salt." So no worries then if global warming is going to take us back to the ice age every winter.

Once nearby Northwich was a major salt centre, beginning

in the 17th century when a search for coal yielded rock salt instead. The Northwich mines eventually collapsed or flooded, but the town still has a salt museum.

Middlewich is now the place where most of the salt used in cooking comes from and there was salt production in Nantwich too.

NINETEEN

A BIG FAIREY

Those who know where to look can still find a little of the old Fairey Aviation factory, where, for example, they turned out Fairey Fulmars for the Fleet Air Arm during the Second World War.

Fairey, now long departed to some airport in the sky, just like much of the British aviation industry, was the creation of a large, smart, passionate, eccentric, man, given to wearing bowler hats, called Charles Richard Fairey. Known as Richard, and born in 1887, at 18 he had been in charge of installing electric lighting in the warehouses and docks of Heysham. He dominated Fairey, which also had bases near London – the land is now part of Heathrow airport – and at Ringway, now Manchester Airport.

Richard Fairey gave to the world the Swordfish (or Stringbag to the men who flew in it), Gannet and Flycatcher, but his company also bequeathed to Cheshire the Fairey Band, sometimes producing brass music at its best, that was part of the life of the Heaton Chapel plant. Founded in 1937 as the Fairey Aviation Works Band, it was one of those manifestations of a northern form of culture that baffles southerners.

Around these parts, brass band enthusiasts are as partisan as football supporters and can be as obsessed as loco spotters and petrolheads. They give up their time to keep their chosen band on the road and they study form and league tables with the intensity normally considered to be the preserve of sports enthusiasts. One company secretary of my acquaintance used to blow away on something in a band when he wasn't attending board meetings and writing minutes. But, as he explained to me, it really is just like football, as he got older his lips were no longer able to impart the power and precision that they once had, he couldn't maintain his place in the team (band) and a career of managing, coaching and spectating was all that was left to him.

Richard Fairey was a Londoner, but he did his bit for the north.

TWENTY

TELEPHONE BOOKS

?

When, many years ago, the celebrated England footballer Len Shackleton included a chapter of his autobiography on the average football director's knowledge of football, he left the page underneath the heading blank.

The same device can be used to illustrate the usefulness of some of Cheshire's telephone directories. It's been suggested that nowhere else in the country are so many people ex directory. Want to call somebody and don't have their number? Not much hope then – even the old journalist's trick of asking an operator to phone the number and see if the person at the other end will take the call doesn't seem to work now.

I've tried asking a few people why it is that they take this line and the answer has sometimes been a very honest, "other people do it, so I thought I would as well." So there's keeping up with the Jones's, Cheshire style for you.

Then there are the people who bar incoming "withheld" numbers. I really can't see the logic in that one. It means that plenty of people who you might actually want to hear from can't get through to you and, yes, it filters out some double glazing and mortgage salespeople as well.

TWENTY-ONE

WIRRAL HOME

The Hundred of Wirral, or the Wirral Peninsula is that bit of the historical county of Cheshire that sticks out at the north west corner between the River Mersey and the River Dee.

The Wirral has its own character, arguably a third sector of the county after the hills and the plain.

One man who loved the area was the broadcaster and naturalist Norman Ellison. In his book, *The Wirral Peninsula* published in 1955 he wrote:-

"For nearly 10 years as 'Nomad the Naturalist' I have broadcast regularly in the BBC's North Regional Children's Hour. I have described the delights of the countryside – the birds and beasts, the trees and flowers – to be seen there. My quest for fresh material has taken me over most parts of the British Isles, yet many of the incidents I have recounted to this cast unseen audience have happened on my own doorstep on Caldy Hill or around the Hilbre Islands I can see as I write these final words. That must be set down to the credit. By birth I am a Lancashire man and proud of it, yet Cheshire has been my home since boyhood. I shall ask nothing better than to pass the rest of my life there; in particular in that part I know and love so well – the Wirral Peninsula."

Ellison also penned copy for the magazine Out of Doors. In the aftermath of the Second World War, this was an inspirational publication encouraging people to get out into the British countryside and explore.

In the autumn 1946 issue Ellison, in a piece entitled, "The Fall of the Year", described how the aroma of burning wood, faint but unmistakable, had tempted him to down his pen, pull on his walking boots, that he called "Gog" and "Magog" and head into the countryside of the Wirral.

"We, my boots and I, knew where we were going," he declared, "for there is only one spot about here from which the fading beauty of the passing year can be seen in all its glory. Somewhere about this time each autumn, we go there and revel in a riot of warm colour such as no words of mine can paint. The way there is along the Green Road, for that is the way by which the old grass grown pedlar's track is known in the village. Mile after mile it meanders up hill and down dale, but always with reasonable straightness. It is broad so that two carriages could pass abreast with ease and the dry-stone walls which bound it are still in good repair although they have weathered the storms of almost two centuries. But today it is a road in name only. A foot-track winds down the centre of it, twisting and turning rounds clumps of gorse and sprawling entanglements of bramble. No wheeled vehicle could travel along it, for man abandoned it when the new turnpike road was opened for coach traffic and nature, as always, has reclaimed her own."

The opportunity would have been welcome to ask Norman Ellison what the impact had been on his devotion to the countryside of his First World War service in The King's Liverpool Regiment, including the Battle of the Somme.

* * *

The fight for liberation of women began early on The Wirral. The Neston Female Friendly Society was founded in 1814 to allow women, left at home with their children, to help each other during the absence of their husbands fighting the French.

The original charter is displayed at the parish church although sadly the word "friendly" was dropped from the title. No doubt there was a good reason for that, but it seems a pity to lose such a pleasant word and despoil a piece of history.

Anyway, the Society's motto remains "Bear ye one another's burdens".

The Society offers benefits to members consisting of :
- sickness benefit
- maternity benefit when the children are born in wedlock
- death grant

Though the committee members are female, the secretary is traditionally a man.

On the first Thursday in June the long standing Ladies Day Walk takes place in Neston, involving a procession from the Malt Shovel pub car park, down the High Street to a service at the church.

After this, the procession heads for Neston Cross for a short service and blessing. It finishes at Neston Civic Hall for tea and the annual general meeting. A truly colourful day is enjoyed.

Norman Ellison drew attention to the custom of "lifting" that in distant times took place in Neston and much father afield. This involved men lifting women and vice versa on different days.

Generally a good time was had by all, but things could get out of hand and this letter appeared in Adams' Weekly Courant on March 26 1771:-

"I cannot but observe a nuisance which seems not to have attracted the notice of the magistrates. I mean the practice of Lifting; or rather, the assembling in a riotous manner of a considerable number (I am sorry to say) at all the gates and other thoroughfares of this City, to extort money from every man whose business may oblige him to pass that way. This is jointly complained of by travellers, who unacquainted with such customs, have given a considerable sum for leave to pursue their journey, and have scarce rode to the other end of the city but must again purchase the liberty of passing on. I should be glad to see so mean a custom abolished by the interposition of authority which cannot fail of adding to the respect due to the magistrates and also to the convenience of every traveller."

TWENTY-TWO

HACKS

When journalists get together the anecdotes come thick and fast. Peter Wheeler, who was an ornament on the Cheshire scene for many years, contributed one to a booklet I helped compile for the late lamented United Co-operatives (an organisation that merged into and became an engine room of The Co-operative Group) to raise funds for Diabetes UK. Peter used to present programmes on BBC Radio Manchester and read the local news on Granada and this anecdote concerns the latter:-

"One of the best-known songs in the musical, Annie Get Your Gun, 'My Defences are Down', offers two vivid images of uselessness, 'Like a knight without his armour, like Samson without his hair.' The newscaster's version of this is to find that you're on the air with nothing to say.

"I spent 12 years reading the news on Granada Television and the night I had nothing to say was no ordinary case of stage fright or amnesia.

"It was in the days before autocue was fixed to the camera to supply the words. The script was printed as hard copy one story to a page. When the Xerox method of duplication came in it was hailed as a great advance on the old, ink-drenched, stencil machines. The print was vivid and much easier to read, but there was one potential problem, you had to use a specific type of paper. If you failed to make the right choice the electrostatic principle of blowing carbon dust over the sheet, creating the image by adhering to the printed area, simply didn't work.

"I rehearsed the bulletin, marvelling at the clarity of the print. It was a routine night until 15 seconds before transmission. I checked the order of the pages, gathered the bundle together and tapped them on the desk to make them tidy. It was then that the incorrect choice of paper made its presence felt. Every word on the 33 pages instantly translated itself into a heap of carbon dust on the studio desk.

"As vision and sound were faded up and we went live, not only did we have nothing to say, but the studio crew were less than sympathetic, having seen me read the bulletin minutes before in rehearsal. As I sat there helplessly because the news is the one show you would be unwise to try and ad-lib, sound and vision were faded out and the viewers were left with only the station ident caption and the repeated signature tune for company, until a replacement script was got into my hands. As we went back on the air, my nerves were in shreds and I was only at the beginning of a 30-minute burble.

"But, look on the bright side, that night made a small contribution to television history because, first thing the following morning, Granada changed its paper supplier.

Peter's not the only one. Rather later I was in the studio as Granada Reports was about to go out when Richard Madeley (not then nationally known) found that he was in a similar position to the one Peter described. However, technology had moved on, in addition there was the luxury of two minutes before on-air time and the problem was solved.

The Cheshire-based freelance, Philip Curtis, contributed to

the same publication and this story concerns drink. Many tales told by journalists involve alcohol and I have Philip's permission to say that he is no exception to this rule:

"For reasons that (perhaps unsurprisingly) are now somewhat obscure, I once spent an evening keeping a red top editor company in his office. While sorting out the world's problems we demolished the best part of a bottle of whisky.

"Outside the newsroom hummed, but nobody came into the great man's office and the phone did not ring. Had Edward Thomas still been around he might have recorded it as a follow-up to 'I Remember Adelstrop': *The steam hissed. Someone cleared his throat, No one left and no one came, On the bare platform. What I saw Was Adlestrop – only the name.*

"As I staggered out into late-night London, I thought to myself that being a national newspaper editor didn't appear to be all that tough a billet. Perhaps I could aspire to those heights.

"The opportunity has, of course, not arisen.

"A predecessor of that Editor had a rather more hands-on approach to his job. Each day, one of his assignments was to pick the next 'Page 3' offering."

Why do journalists drink? Despite, these days, not having as much time to do it as they used to. The theory is often put forward that it has much to do with the waiting around that the job can entail. I take the view that another cause is the clash of personalities that is often required. So there can be a demand for the mental toughness to knock on a door and ask the immediately bereaved for a photograph or seek an interview with someone whose company went bust an hour ago; then the hack switches into rather more sensitive mode to create a minor literary work out of the material that has been obtained.

TWENTY-THREE

OLD SOLDIERS

There was a sad moment for Cheshire in 2007 when the local regiment became part of the Mercians. Up until then, The Cheshire Regiment had been one of the very few in the British Army never to be amalgamated.

With a history dating back to the 17th century and battle honours including South Africa 1900-02, Somme, Arras and El Alamein, the regiment was mourned by many in the county.

There was, too, the Cheshire Yeomanry, that reckoned to be one of the last units of the British army to fight on horseback. They were founded by a chap from Tabley at the end of the 18th century.

What pictures of the good folk of Cheshire and elsewhere are conjured by "Yeomanry". My 1926 dictionary, always worth consulting alongside more modern ones, explains that in early English history a yeoman was a common menial attendant, "but after the 15th century one of a class of small freeholders, forming the next grade below gentleman; a man of small estate or small farmer or countryman above the grade of labourer; an officer of the royal household; a member of the yeomanry cavalry."

So, middle class I guess, with a hint of blue collar.

The early history of the Yeomanry of Cheshire was not entirely glorious. A prominent part was played in the "Peterloo" massacre of August 16 1819 in Manchester, when a public meeting on parliamentary reform was broken up and at least 11 people died, with many more injured.

More orthodox military work came later and the first battle honour was awarded for service in South Africa at the end of Queen Victoria's reign.

TWENTY-THREE
HAZEL GROVE HEINKEL

In the course of some research in the 1990s I found myself exchanging letters and having phone conversations with Wing Commander Christopher Deanesly, a wartime RAF pilot.

He was an extrovert character and if the phone rang, one of the children answered and there was then the sound of giggling, I would guess that an announcement that "Wing Commander Deanesly wants to speak to you" would follow.

Christopher was known as "Jumbo" in the RAF and he was indeed a big man, considering that he had flown Spitfires and was probably the only allied airman to find himself in the English Channel twice during the Battle of Britain and survive. How he managed to extricate himself habitually in haste from the confines of a Spitfire cockpit was not at all clear to all who knew him. "Jumbo" also had the misfortune to own a name that is constantly misspelt – so "note to sub" as journalists say – it really is Deanesly. The explanation for the name, so he told me, was that his grandfather had been Mr Sly and had much disliked that affliction. So, when he married Miss Deane, the opportunity was taken to combine the appellations.

One day on the phone Hazel Grove was mentioned and then the coin dropped all round. A few hundred yards from my house was the spot (on the edge of what is now Stockport Golf Club) where a German Heinkel bomber crashed on the night of May 7/8 1941. This was claimed to be the only German aircraft to fall in the Greater Manchester area during the war and Jumbo and his New Zealand air gunner, Sergeant Jack Scott, also a Battle of Britain veteran, were the victors, flying in a Boulton Paul Defiant.

At the time, this incident caused considerable excitement in the area and it is well remembered today.

The Stockport Express reported a few days after the event:

"A solicitor armed with an axe was among a party of four men, who rounded up a member of the crew of a German bomber ------ and he gave a graphic description of seeing the 'plane, a mass of flames, hurtling to the ground.

"'I was standing out-of-doors talking to a friend, another solicitor," he said, 'and we commented that the shells from the guns seemed to concentrate in one spot. Then we discerned what looked like a ball of flame and as it dropped we could see it was a 'plane on fire. It seemed to fall a short distance away from us and we ran for my car. With two wardens we hurried to where we thought it had dropped.

'"Leaving the car in a farmyard we separated to search for any surviving members of the crew, but scarcely had we moved when one of the wardens called that they had found a man. The German had given up his revolver and we took him to the car. He was a young Bavarian and we brought him back to my home and telephoned the police.'"

The "Young Bavarian" was the aircraft's radio operator and he told his captors that it was his 21st birthday. He partook of tea and sandwiches while the police were awaited. All of the crew parachuted to safety across Cheadle, Bramhall and Hazel Grove.

It was reported that hundreds of people journeyed to see the wreckage.

Deanesly and Scott were one of the most successful night fighter teams at the time and soon afterwards one received the DFC and the other (being an NCO) the DFM.

Jack Scott came from Auckland and had been in farming and a sailor with the Union Steamship company before the war. He returned to New Zealand in 1943. After his release from the Air Force he became a builder and spent two years working on a hospital in the New Hebrides, now Vanuatu, in the south Pacific. Back in New Zealand again he ran a joinery shop and later a hardware store. He died in 1999.

I never knew Jack but, as can be gathered, I remember Jumbo with affection. Later in the war he commanded a squadron of Dakota transport aircraft and flew one, towing a glider, during the Rhine Crossing in 1945. After the war he became a successful businessman.

In old age mobility became a problem and he obtained an electric buggy in which he would rush around the streets of his home town, sometimes venturing a considerable distance. There were occasions when he was over enthusiastic and the buggy would be tipped up. The usual scenario was that people would rush to Jumbo's aid and an ambulance would be called – but as soon as the veteran pilot was back on his wheels he would zoom off and the blood wagon would, I'm afraid, have a fruitless journey.

In 1998 the man always associated in these parts with the destruction of the Hazel Grove Heinkel died aged 88 and I wrote a short piece for the Stockport Express, bringing that story to a close.

Manchester and the surrounding area did suffer plenty of carnage at the hands of the Germans during the Second World War, notably in the "Manchester Blitz", just before Christmas 1940, when an excellent film was made by the CWS film unit. The title, "Manchester Took it Too", does rather hint at a northern inferiority complex that can be amusing to southerners.

A few days before the triumph of Deanesly and Scott, another Defiant crew had downed another Heinkel, that fell near Northwich.

One of the RAF bases from which Manchester, Liverpool and Cheshire were protected by night fighters was at Cranage, not far from Knutsford, which is where this other crew were based. Also in the vicinity was a factory producing Wellington bombers, that would make their first flight from Cranage.

A night fighter squadron CO at Cranage for a time was "Boozy" Kellett, whose drinking, actually doesn't seem to have been above the norm for RAF aircrew at the time, but such nicknames can frequently be far from complimentary and are not always accurate.

In 1944 the United States Army Air Force came to Cranage, no doubt able to impress the locals with ample supplies of chocolate, nylons and other goodies generally denied to wartime Britons.

A Stockport inhabitant who had been a railway fireman during the war explained to me one of the techniques for sharing in the Yank bounty.

My informant had sometimes been allocated to the footplate of locomotives hauling newly arrived Americans away from Liverpool docks. The trick, as the train was waiting to depart, was for fireman and driver to make themselves look as scruffy, depressed and generally war weary as possible and then to walk solemnly down the loaded train, clearly intent on some important contribution to the war effort, yet, at the same time, weighed down by the general awfulness of the lot of being British.

On the return journey to the footplate the pair were still weighed down, but now by the abundance of presents that had been heaped upon them by concerned GIs.

A story of Manchester's Christmas blitz came to me from a work colleague many years ago. In 1940 he was a teenager living on the north side of the city. On December 22 he and his younger sister were despatched across to the Cheshire side to visit an aunt and collect a vase that was intended for their mother.

On the way back the bombing had started and, as the bus reached the centre of the city, an inspector instructed the driver to go no further. Roy and his sister spent the night sheltering in cellars and anywhere else that presented itself.

The next morning they reached home to find their mother, not unreasonably, in a very distressed state, but not only were Roy and his sister safe, but they were able to present mum proudly with the vase, still in pristine condition.

The ornament survived, but over those two nights, the centre of Manchester suffered. And several hundred people killed. The Free Trade Hall was virtually destroyed, so was the Mitchell Memorial Hall and there was significant damage to the Royal Exchange, the Corn Exchange and the Cathedral. Now the flame window in the Manchester Regiment chapel commemorates the bombing of the Cathedral and the city as a whole.

TWENTY-FOUR

PLAYING A ROUND

For two and a half years I earned money at golf. I was at school and my weekend job was caddying at the Shooters Hill club on the border between London and Kent. I remember a player with one arm, who could hit the ball longer distances than most of his fellows with two arms and, though I didn't witness it, there was the time when a member achieved a hole in one, went straight from the 18th green to his car and wasn't seen around the place for six months.

Legend has it that on his return the steward presented him with a bill for all the drinks that had been placed on his account in his absence – a considerable punishment for failing to buy the traditional round to celebrate his achievement.

Unusually, I never got the bug and have never played a single hole in my life, but that's a pity in one way because Cheshire is well endowed with golf courses.

There's Mere, for instance, near Knutsford, described as "the Wentworth of the north" by a TV commentator, Peover (though please pronounce it "Peever") with its natural water features and the heathland course at Delamere Forest, little changed in the 100 years since it was created.

Then there's Lymm, with the Manchester Ship Canal running alongside, Upton-by-Chester, "visitors and societies are welcome throughout the week and at weekends – available tee times permitting" and Prestbury, opened in 1920 and designed by Harry Shapland Colt, who, we are told, "is often described as the Sir Christopher Wren of golf course architects". Come to think of it I've heard three people say that this week.

Hoylake, the links course, on the Wirral, mustn't be forgotten, to which the Open Championship returned in 2006 for the first time since 1967.

That's just a taster – golf balls fly all across Cheshire.

TWENTY-FIVE

SWEET ENDINGS

Chocolate is one of the big delicacies of the moment around here, with Simon Dunn intent on fattening up Cheshire from his various shops. And from one big chain you can buy his Cheshire Chocolate Porter, brewed by Frederic Robinson at the Unicorn Brewery in Stockport. Not to everyone's taste I imagine, but I could make out the chocolate and that made it to my taste.